Editor
Gisela Lee

Managing Editor
Karen Goldfluss, M.S. Ed.

Editor-in-Chief
Sharon Coan, M.S. Ed.

Illustrator
Sue Fullam
Linda Myers, M.A. Ed. (Interior
Art Concepts)

Cover Artist
Lesley Palmer

Art Coordinator
Denice Adorno

Imaging
Alfred Lau
Ralph Olmedo, Jr.

Product Manager
Phil Garcia

Publisher
Mary D. Smith, M.S. Ed.

Art&Artists

OF 20th CENTURY AMERICA

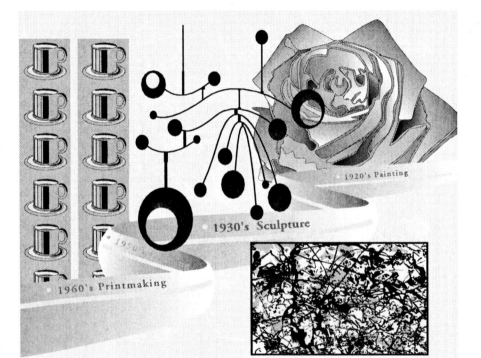

1920's Painting

1930's Sculpture

1960's Printmaking

Author

Linda A. Myers, M.A. Ed. & Judith Stedman

Teacher Created Resources

Teacher Created Resources, Inc.
6421 Industry Way
Westminster, CA 92683
www.teachercreated.com.
ISBN: 978-0-7439-3087-1
©2001 Teacher Created Resources, Inc.
Reprinted, 2007
Made in U.S.A.

Table of Contents

Introduction

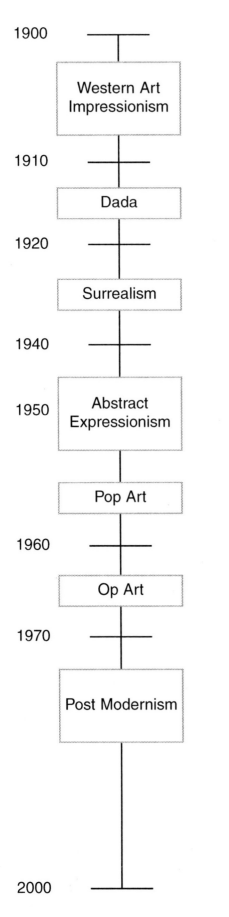

Art Environment

Art should be an important part of every child's education. Children should be exposed to the different types of art forms and artists so maybe one day they could be a Vincent Van Gogh, Dorothea Lange, or a Diego Rivera of their generation. For this reason, this book provides a variety of opportunities for students to explore the many mediums of art.

Along with teaching art, teachers need to provide an environment or classroom art museum that promotes exploration of art, not only through activities, but through self-exploration of artists, mediums, and styles.

If there is not a space for an art center, a plastic storage chest can be used to store all the supplies and art works. Place a decorated sign with "Art" written on it on the chest. If you put the chest under a window or empty wall, you have created a mini art center.

The important thing to remember is that, in order for students to value art, the teachers must make art an important part of his or her curriculum. This may be a task that is often not easy to accomplish or realize but still worth attempting.

Room Environment

Setting up a room can add dramatically to the success of any activity. Not every classroom has the room or space to put up elaborate displays to go with every unit that is taught. On the next page are several ideas that can be used as a yearlong activity or some that can be used for a short period of time. It is the hope that you will take one or more of the activities listed on the next page and make it your own. The success of any activity depends on the ingenuity or creativity of students.

Introduction *(cont.)*

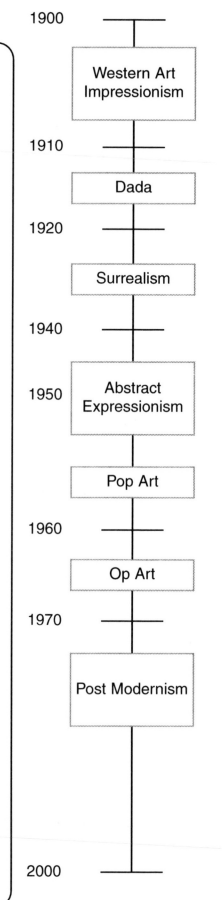

1900

Western Art Impressionism

1910

Dada

1920

Surrealism

1940

1950

Abstract Expressionism

Pop Art

1960

Op Art

1970

Post Modernism

2000

Room Environment *(cont.)*

- Display articles, pictures, and items that represent each artist's time frame.

- Provide a blank timeline template that the class will use at the end of its unit to show important events, people, inventions, and fashions. If the class is doing more than one time frame, the timeline could be put at the end of the each era studied so that students see the development of American history through the use of a timeline.

- Play music of the period of the artist the class is studying.

- Discuss why the artist and his or her work are remembered. Have students write biographies on various artists and/or give oral reports. Use the Art Resources listed on pages 100–102 as possible references.

- Have students make a timeline of the life of the artist they are studying. Go over different kinds of timelines that they could use. Encourage them to use their own imagination and develop their own unique timeline. Similarly, a classroom timeline can be placed on a bulletin board. Using the timeline cards provided on pages 103–112 and the direct quotes provided at the end of each unit, students can create a classroom timeline as each artist, art style, and/or time period is discussed in class.

- Have an open house to display information about an artist or a group of artists. Have students dress in costumes representing the various decades that the artists lived in or represented.

- Invite other classes to visit your class to learn about the different artists. Choose students to act as docents to the students from the other classes.

- Participate in a live wax museum. Have each student select an artist that they enjoyed learning about and dress up as that artist. During an open house or presentation, visitors press an imaginary button and the "artist" comes alive and tells the listener about his or her life.

- Students tape record a biography about each artist and play it back using a tape recorder provided under each artist's works as classes go through a student-made museum. Students can stop at each artist station and play the tape recording and learn more about each artist.

Introduction (cont.)

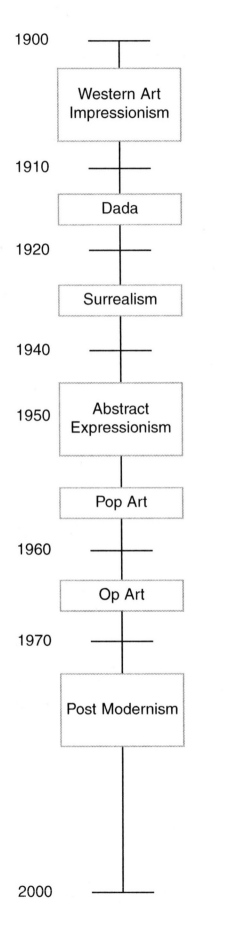

1900 — Western Art Impressionism

1910 — Dada

1920 — Surrealism

1940 — Abstract Expressionism

1950 — Abstract Expressionism

1960 — Pop Art

Op Art

1970 — Post Modernism

2000 —

Does Art Imitate History or Does History Imitate Art?

The twentieth century has been a period of enormous change in visual arts. Art which includes graffiti, found objects, or photography has permeated print, journalism, television, computer graphics, advertising, film, and fashion.

It is the intent of this book to introduce American artists of the 20th century who have documented American history through their art. To gain a better understanding of art and its history, teachers should help students reflect on key historical events of the last 100 years. Using an interdisciplinary approach, teachers can help students gain a better understanding of how the past impacts the present.

This book includes a timeline that presents an informative look at some notable people, innovative ideas, and important events of the past 100 years. Artists who have made an impact in their chosen medium from various cultural backgrounds and art movements have been selected. These artists have taken the path less traveled to express their thoughts and ideas. They were unique for their time in the following mediums: film, photography, sculpture, textiles, printmaking, painting, illustration, and graphic design.

Photography and film have allowed people to look at history as it is being made. Cameras capture the moment, letting the viewer understand more fully the impact history can have on people. Painters and sculptures record history as they see it. Whether abstractly or in a realistic setting, color, shape, and form can set the mood.

Twenty American artists have been grouped by using a timeline that parallels major historical events with their artistic interpretation. This book includes art lessons, biographies, extended activities, and resources for further exploration of the artists and different mediums of each time period.

Hopefully, the biographies and activities will help students answer the question, "Does art imitate history or does history imitate art?"

New Media Extended Activities

Here are suggestions for student activities that incorporate multimedia equipment and software.

Materials

Hardware: computer, scanner, Internet access, printer
Software: *Photoshop®, HyperCard®, Gif Animator®, Paintshop®* (painting software)

Animation

Students scan images from flipbook projects to hypercard animation software using *Gif Animator* software. They color the frames (at least 5 frames) using special effects and then animate.

Film

Students search the Internet for sites about George Lucas, featuring one of his famous films featuring a super hero.

Each student reports to class the most interesting site he or she found. Each student should be ready to tell class how he or she found the site and why he or she found it interesting. Each student draws a super hero, using paint software and then prints, frames, and displays the drawing.

Mobile

A student videotapes a close-up of a moving object that would not be recognizable by other students. Present the video to the class. Have them guess the origin.

Mural

Students search the Internet for mural sites from various cultures. They note differences and similarities of colors and surface. Using *PaintShop* or *PhotoShop* software, students practice using a variety of brush strokes.

Photography

Each student takes a photo of a child or adult on a digital camera and scans it into *PhotoShop* and distorts it to become a household pet. A regular camera can also be used and each student can simply scan the photo into *PhotoShop*. Print, frame, give it a name, and display it.

Pop Art

Students scan a label of a famous product into the computer. After the product label is scanned in *PaintShop*, make a different name for the product. Print, frame, and display it.

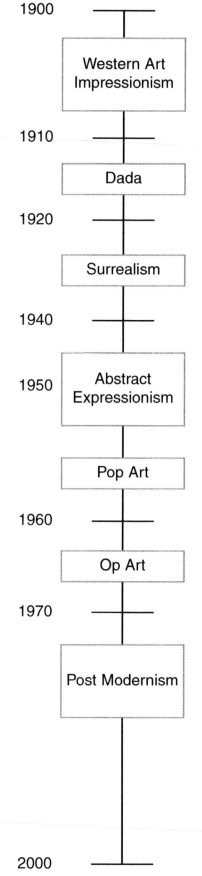

1900	
	Western Art Impressionism
1910	
	Dada
1920	
	Surrealism
1940	
1950	Abstract Expressionism
	Pop Art
1960	
	Op Art
1970	
	Post Modernism
2000	

1900s at a Glance

The first decade of the 20th century was highlighted by the election of President William McKinley in 1900. Unfortunately, it also witnessed the assassination of President McKinley the following year which led Vice President Teddy Roosevelt to the oval office. That same year, England's Queen Victoria died and marked the end of the Victorian Era which began in 1837. This decade also witnessed the conclusion of the Boer War and social and political upheaval that led to the Boxer Rebellion in China.

Not only was this a time of political changes, it was also a time of growth and scientific inventions and advancements. Henry Ford created the Model T in 1908, as well as introducing the idea of mass production to the industrial world. Orville and Wilbur Wright introduced flight to the world while Albert Einstein published his theory of relativity of time and space. It was also during this era that Sigmund Freud's *The Interpretation of Dreams* was published. In 1904 Robert Scott was the first person to reach the South Pole while in 1909 Robert Peary and his assistant Matthew Henson were the first to reach the North Pole.

In the meantime immigrants were flocking to America in the early 1900s in hopes of a better life for themselves and their families. The "American Dream" became a reality for many while others continued to look for their dream. By 1909 the U.S. population reached 92 million.

For children, Boy Scouts was brought to America by businessman William D. Boyce. While touring England, he came into contact with the Boy Scouts of England. He was impressed with their organization, which was founded on the principles of teaching young men leadership and good citizenship.

This decade also marked the occasion of honoring and recognizing mothers. Anna Jarvis started the movement to recognize mothers in 1908 and by 1914 President Woodrow Wilson signed a resolution recognizing Mother's Day as a national holiday on the second Sunday of May.

The turn of the new century was a time for people to reflect on the past and dream of the new and exciting opportunities awaiting them. There was a sense of hope and promise. The future seemed to hold so many new beginnings for immigrants, scientific advancements, and social changes.

Eadweard Muybridge   1830–1904

Eadweard Muybridge, the father of motion photography, was born in Kingston-on-Thames, England, in 1830. He had taken the strange name Eadweard Muybridge in the belief that it was the Anglo-Saxon original of his real name, Edward James Muggeridge. In California he photographed the Pacific Coast for the government, accompanied the official expedition to Alaska when the territory was acquired from Russia in 1867, and became a specialist in industrial photography.

The art of motion photography might very well be said to have gotten its start because of a horse named Occidental. Leland Stanford, the former governor of California asked Eadweard Muybridge to help him learn how a horse moved through the use of photography. Using what was known as a "wet plate," Muybridge was able to make a silhouette of the horse in motion. He proved that all four feet of a horse leave the ground at the same time during a gallop. This information not only changed the way artists drew horses, but it was quite helpful to physicians, veterinarians, and others interested in animal and human motion.

Muybridge continued his study of motion in animals but eventually became more interested in the motion of humans. He began studying athletes running, jumping, rowing, and walking. His work created the illusion of motion and is considered the link between still photography and cinema giving him the title of the father of motion pictures. Through a unique projection method, Muybridge was able to animate his photos, creating the first motion picture.

Muybridge was an inventor as well as a photographer. In 1869 he invented one of the first shutters for a camera and continued working on improving photographic equipment throughout his life.

In his final years, he toured the United States and Europe lecturing about his studies. He would use the hundreds of photographs he had taken of men, women, children, and animals to demonstrate this new kind of photographic technique.

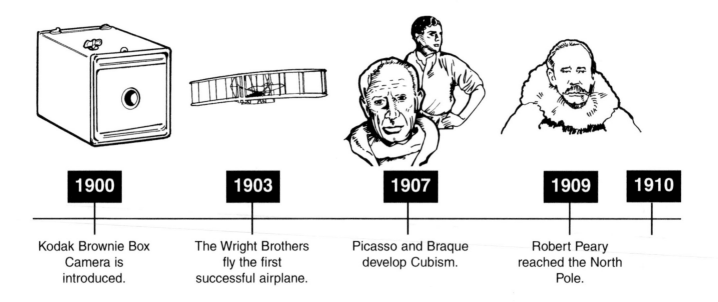

1900	1903	1907	1909	1910
Kodak Brownie Box Camera is introduced.	The Wright Brothers fly the first successful airplane.	Picasso and Braque develop Cubism.	Robert Peary reached the North Pole.	

Motion Flipbook

Related Areas

Art

Language Arts

Science

Social Studies

Focus

Students study motion.

Activity

making a flip book of motion

Vocabulary

motion, locomotion, camera, animation, projection

Materials

3" x 8" strips of white construction paper; pencil; colored pencils; crayons; examples of Muybridge's work; chart paper; transparency; pipe cleaners; straws; 4" x 6" plain index card; hard wood mannequin; clay; ziplock plastic bags

Implementation

Day 1

1. Introduce students to Eadweard Muybridge. Show examples of his work.
2. Explain to students that they are going to become movie makers.
3. Take students to observe people in motion at recess or during a physical education class.

Day 2

1. Using a wooden mannequin, demonstrate movement.
2. Students use pipe cleaners and straws to make 3 to 5 figures in different positions (i.e., sitting, bending, playing soccer, jumping). Use small balls of clay for stands.
3. Students draw pictures of their pipe cleaner figures of each movement. They should look like stick figures.
4. With a pencil students draw a little picture on each righthand page. They make each drawing just a little different from the previous page. Students must press hard to make an impression of their drawing on the underneath side of their page. Using the impression of the drawing as a guide, students can draw in the lines.

Day 3

1. Review day 1 activities emphasizing movement of figures.
2. Pass out 1 sheet of paper and have students divide paper in half vertically.
3. Divide class into groups of 4. Each student from a group stands up and takes a turn striking a 3-minute action pose. Students draw stick figures of the pose. Divide paper into 4 equal sections, using both sides for 4 poses. Emphasize that the stick figure should fill each section.

Motion Flipbook *(cont.)*

Implementation *(cont.)*

Day 4

1. Demonstrate to the class the steps involved in making a flip book. Print steps on chart paper or have steps written on a transparency or chalkboard.

2. Pass out ziplock bags to each group containing pipe cleaners, index cards, clay, and straws in various sizes.

3. Pass out four 4" x 8" pieces of white construction paper. Have students make a flip book by folding each piece in half and stacking it on top of three other pieces of paper. Staple all pages together in the middle at least two times.

4. Draw an object on each right-hand side. Each drawing should be slightly different than the object before it. Press down hard as you draw so that an impression is left on the page underneath the page you're working on. The impression will leave the student's image at the same spot on each page. Students trace over the impression.

5. Each drawing should gradually show a movement of the figure or something happening to the figure (i.e., hand moving to mouth, fish eating another fish, etc.).

6. Students color each picture with colored pencils or crayons. Have students share their flip books with the rest of the class.

Extended Activities

1. Give students an 8" x 3" strip of construction paper for a thumbprint comic strip. Have students divide the strip into 4 equal squares, using a pencil and a ruler. Provide washable ink pads so students can make thumbprint characters (i.e., birds, insects, animals, people). Show motion by drawing lines on characters.

2. Students cut out figures from newspapers or magazines showing movement through some sports activity. Students make a collage of figures to show different kinds of movement. Mount them on paper and display on a bulletin board.

3. Students write a poem on motion.

"Occidental was trotting past me at the rate of 2.27, accurately timed. . . the exposure. . . being less than 1/1000 part of a second. . . . The picture has been retouched, as is customary at this time with all first-class photographic work, for the purpose of giving a better effect to the details. In every other respect, the photograph is exactly as it was made in the camera."

Eadweard Muybridge

Frederic Remington   **1861–1909**

Frederic Remington is best known for his romantic portrayal of the West as it once was, before cities and people took over. Remington was born in Canton in northern New York on October 4, 1861. His boyhood fostered a lifelong love of horses and the outdoors, while his father's tales of action as a cavalry officer in the Civil War inspired a passion for things military.

Remington studied art at the Yale Art School. He left to roam the Dakotas, Montana, the Arizona Territory, and Texas to document an era that was fast vanishing. He illustrated Theodore Roosevelt's book *Ranch Life and Hunting Trail*.

Remington concentrated on the last days of the cowboys of the far West. After 1900 he developed an impressionistic style that he executed on his landscapes and still kept his realistic style to his figures in sculpture and paintings.

During a career that spanned less than 25 years, Frederic Remington, produced a huge body of work, illustrations, paintings, sculptures, and works of fiction and nonfiction—the vast majority of it centered on the West. His influence shaped the popular imagination of the West.

Remington had been exhibiting in major art shows since 1888 and was seeking recognition as not just an illustrator, but as an artist in the recognized sense of the term. He made the breakthrough he was seeking in 1895 when he turned to sculpting, which he excelled at and which earned him the critical respect for his work that he strive for. He completed 22 sculptures, many which became the defining masterpieces of the Western art tradition. When he died at the age of 48, a victim of appendicitis, his epitaph simply stated: "He knew the horse."

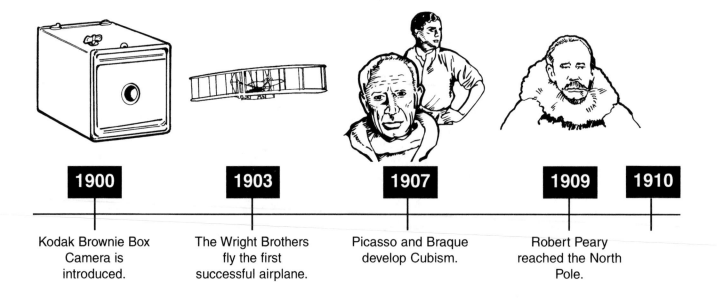

1900	**1903**	**1907**	**1909**	**1910**
Kodak Brownie Box Camera is introduced.	The Wright Brothers fly the first successful airplane.	Picasso and Braque develop Cubism.	Robert Peary reached the North Pole.	

Sculpting a Horse

Related Areas

Art

Language Arts

Science

Focus

Students create three-dimensional sculptures.

Activity

sculpting a horse

Vocabulary

armature, three-dimensional, skeleton, patina, base, form, space, balance, rhythm

Materials

thin, flexible, galvanized wire; wire cutters or sharp scissors; pliers; clay; sticks, nail file, toothbrush, etc., for modeling clay; pencils; drawing paper

Implementation

Day 1

1. Introduce students to Remington. Show examples of his work.
2. Explain to students that they are going to become sculptors.
3. Show a video and have pictures to demonstrate horses in motion. Show examples from Muybridge.
4. Students draw stick figures of a horse from photos.

Day 2

1. Use a wooden mannequin to demonstrate movement.
2. Students build an armature. Cut the wire into many short pieces, 2–3" long. Bend and double the wire as if you were drawing a stick figure of a horse. Use pliers to twist the wire well at the joints. As the armature is built, capture movement and expression as Remington did. Keep turning the armature as you work to view it from all sides. Is the armature balanced? Is the rhythm right?
3. Wrap wire around and around the armature to make the shapes stronger and more bulky. This will keep the legs and neck from becoming wobbly as you add the clay. It is very important that you take your time here and build a sturdy armature.

Sculpting a Horse *(cont.)*

Implementation *(cont.)*

Day 2 *(cont.)*

4. Once the armature is complete, adhere/nail it down to a wooden base. Add the clay. A sculptor works on a turntable at eye level. You can make your own turntable by placing a small board on top of a stack of magazines.

5. Warm the clay in your fingers before working with it. Add the clay to the armature to fill in the body.

6. Add the clay evenly to the armature. Work all over and all around. Do not finish one part before the rest.

Extended Activities

Making a Sculpture with a Patina

1. Create a more professional model using plaster of paris. Dip the horse armature into plaster, a part at a time. Let the plaster dry for 2 days.

2. Use sand paper for details and finishing touches. Allow the sculpture to dry for 2 more days before you add the patina.

3. You add color to the plaster by washing it in diluted water colors or wiping on shoe polish (make sure there is good ventilation). Finally, polish the patina surface with paste wax and find a suitable base upon which to mount the finished horse.

Extended Technology Activity

1. Using the Internet, students research cattle brands. Students see that although each brand is different, there are certain symbols used by everyone. Generally, the owner's initials or the ranch name appear in the brand.

2. Using a graphics program like *Adobe Photoshop*, students use their own initials and design their own brand.

"I knew the railroad was coming—I saw men already swarming into the land. . . . I knew the wild riders and the vacant land were about to vanish forever, and the more I considered the subject the bigger the forever loomed.

Without knowing exactly how to do it, I began to try to record some facts around me, and the more I looked, the more the panorama unfolded. . . . I saw the living, breathing end of three American centuries of smoke and dust and sweat, and I now see quite another thing where it all took place, but it does not appeal to me."

Frederic Remington

1910s at a Glance

The 1910s saw the beginning and end of a world war, the addition of two new states, the sinking of the *Titanic*, and the role of women in politics becoming more pronounced.

In Europe what began as a local war between Austria-Hungary and Serbia, eventually turned into a global war involving 32 nations. World War I lasted four years with the world viewing the heroics and horrors of what warfare entailed. Legends like The Red Baron and Mata Hari were remembered in song as well as romanticized in stories and even cartoons by their enemies as well as their own countrymen.

On the home front, other important changes were taking place. Arizona and New Mexico became states in 1912. Woodrow Wilson was elected president in 1912. In 1915 the first fighter plane was constructed, and Henry Ford developed a farm tractor. Jeannette Rankin became the first woman elected to the U.S. Congress. In 1919 the 18th Amendment to the U.S. Constitution was ratified. This amendment prohibited the making, buying, and selling of alcoholic beverages. This amendment was repealed in 1933 by the 21st Amendment of the Constitution.

Paradoxically, while most people of the world were embroiled in war, the world of arts and entertainment began to make enormous strides. Pablo Picasso and Claude Monet were becoming celebrated artists of their time. Hollywood established itself as the center of the motion picture industry and such box office draws as Charlie Chaplin and Mary Pickford were among the most recognizable faces in the world. The first jazz recordings were made during this decade too.

Meanwhile in the sports world, the first national baseball game was played in 1917. Jim Thorpe won two gold medals in the 1912 Olympics. Thorpe became known as one of the most talented men in sports history. Not only was he a great runner, he went on to play both baseball and football and won awards in both sports.

This was also the era which marked the first observation of Haley's Comet, protons and electrons were first detected, the true dimensions of the Milky Way were discerned, and the architecture of Frank Lloyd Wright became popular.

The decade, like most times, was filled with contradictions, from the lives of the very wealthy—such as those who traveled on luxury liners like the *Titanic*—to the millions of immigrants who lived in poverty. America dreamed of better times while, for the first time in it history, more of its people lived in cities than in the rural areas that were once the backbone of the country. Perhaps, most ironically, the United States entered the Great War under the leadership of one the century's most significant pacifists, President Woodrow Wilson.

Alfred Stieglitz   1864–1946

Alfred Stieglitz was the most respected photographer of his time to fight for the recognition of photography as a valid art form. He took pictures in a time when photography was considered only scientific curiosity and not art. This battle would last his whole life. In 1923 he was asked if he would give the Museum of Fine Arts some of his photographs. This was significant because it was the first time that a major American art museum included photographs for display. In 1924 Stieglitz sent 27 photographs to the Metropolitan Museum of Art. He was the first photographer to reach this achievement in America. His work became a standard for all photography in the United States.

In 1883, at the age of 19, he took his first pictures while attending a school in Berlin. He was fascinated by the medium and started to experiment with new techniques, pushing the limits that were the standards at that time. He was told that a camera could only be used in the daytime. He decided to challenge the theory and set up his camera in a small cellar. The cellar was lit only by a weak electric light bulb and focused on a dynamo. He made a 24-hour exposure that resulted in a perfect negative. This negative effectively rebuked the necessity of daylight. Later in his life, Stieglitz took the first successful "rainy day," "snow storm," and "night" photographs.

His style began to change with his new environment. He turned away from the picturesque themes that he used in Europe. He began to photograph the unfashionable. In 1922, at the age of 58, Alfred Stieglitz took 10 photographs of clouds, thus beginning a project that would occupy his attention for the next several years. Clouds, after all, were "there for everyone—no tax as yet on them," and surely no one could accuse him of hypnotizing something that moved so freely across the sky. Several other reasons clearly also motivated Stieglitz to study clouds, for he continued to photograph them almost every summer when he was at his home in Lake George, New York, until he stopped working in 1937. He made more than 300 finished studies of clouds, far more than of any subject other than his wife, Georgia O'Keeffe.

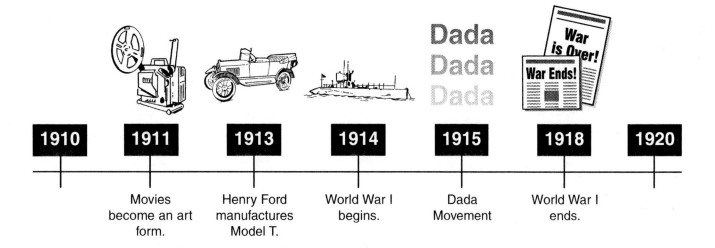

1910	1911	1913	1914	1915	1918	1920
	Movies become an art form.	Henry Ford manufactures Model T.	World War I begins.	Dada Movement	World War I ends.	

Photography

Related Areas

Art

Language Arts

Science

Social Studies

Focus

Students study the beauty of nature through photography.

Activity

making a collage of photographs of one subject

Vocabulary

camera, photography, still life, landscape, contrast

Materials

disposable black and white camera; 35 mm camera with black and white film; 5" x 5" white frame with 4" x 4" hole; paper scissors; glue; a variety of color and black and white nature photos from magazines

Implementation

Day 1

1. Introduce students to Alfred Stieglitz. Show examples of his nature photography and those of other photographers (Ansel Adams) who include nature photographs in their major works.
2. Students will compose one 4" x 4" collage of one subject in nature.
3. Students select photographs from magazines and arrange. Then they glue them on a sheet of construction paper. The collage will become their photograph.

Day 2

1. Give each student a 4" x 4" frame, which he or she will use to view his or her subject through. Using white frames, students go outside and choose 4 square inches of nature (e.g., sky, clouds, grass, trees).
2. Take students on one short field trip outdoors. The amount of time for this activity depends on the flexibility of the schedule and whether parent volunteers or aides can help. Help students use this frame to really focus in on what they are really seeing. This activity will also help prepare them for taking their actual 4 photographs of the same subject on 4 different days. Once back in the room, discuss how viewing through a frame allows you to focus on a subject without distractions. Light, space, and balance are also more clearly defined.

Photography (cont.)

Implementation (cont.)

Days 3–5

Review the past two days' activities. Review how the frame helped focus on their subject. Explain that a camera is like a frame. It allows the photographer to focus in on the subject, choose the distance, as well as balance what he or she needs in the photograph with what is not necessary. Once the photographs are developed, return photos to each students and have them select their best photograph to be framed. Frame these photographs. Possible framing material would be black construction paper, foam board, posterboard, or matting board. (Check frame stores for discounts to teachers.) Display photographs in class, local art gallery, or library, or, better yet, in a prominent place in your school.

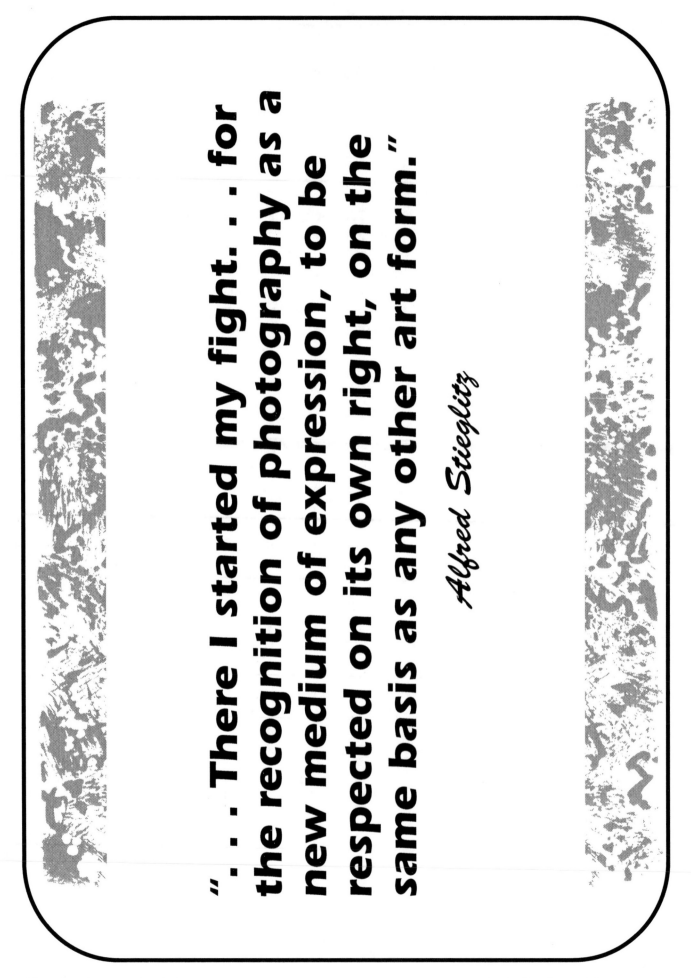

". . . There I started my fight. . . for the recognition of photography as a new medium of expression, to be respected on its own right, on the same basis as any other art form."

Alfred Stieglitz

Frank Lloyd Wright   1867–1959

Frank Lloyd Wright is regarded as one of the most influential figures in modern Western architecture. His radically innovative designs, utilizing a building style based on natural forms, organic architecture, have made him stand out as the major American architect of our times.

Frank Lloyd Wright was born in Richland Center, Wisconsin, June 8, 1867, and died on April 9, 1959. That he continued working right up to the time of his death is a measure of his passion and commitment to his field.

Why is Frank Lloyd Wright important? Do you have a living room in your house? Or a carport? Does your house have an "open" floor plan? Is so, then the way you live is being directly influenced by Frank Lloyd Wright's innovations in residential architecture. Drawing inspiration from his native Midwestern prairie, he challenged Americans to trade their box-like houses for wide-open living spaces. Mr. Wright's "organic architecture" was a radical departure from the traditional architecture of his day, which was dominated by European styles that dated back hundreds of years or even millennia. His architectural designs were initially more symmetrical, reaching out toward some real or imagined expansive horizon. The architecture of these houses served as the inspirational source for the Prairie School.

In contrast to the openness of those houses and as if in conflict with their immediate city environment, Wright's urban buildings tend to be walled in with light entering primarily from above, through skylights. With his reputation assured on both sides of the Atlantic, Wright proclaimed that the structural principles found in natural forms should guide modern American architecture. He praised the virtues of an organic architecture that would use reinforced concrete in the configurations found in seashells and snails and would build skyscrapers the way trees were formed; that is, with a central "trunk" deeply rooted in the ground.

Wright's view of architecture was essentially romantic. His efforts in the time of mass production (modular planning and prefabrication), seemed halfhearted at best. The most spectacular buildings of his mature period were based on forms borrowed from nature, and the intentions were clearly romantic, poetic, and intensely personal. Examples of these buildings are the following: Tokyo's Imperial Hotel (1915–1922); Fallingwater (Kaugmann House, 1936), Mill Run, Pennsylvania; the SC Johnson and Son Wax Company Administration Center (1935–1950), Racine, Wisconsin; Taliesin West (1938–1959); and New York City's Guggenheim Museum (completed 1959). Frank Lloyd Wright has left a rich heritage of completed buildings throughout the United States.

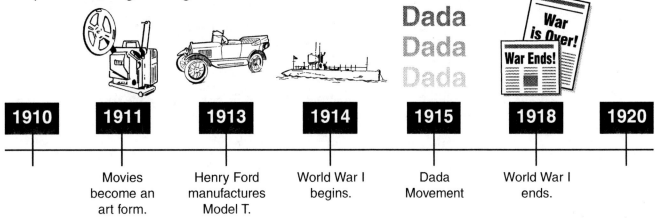

1910	1911	1913	1914	1915	1918	1920
	Movies become an art form.	Henry Ford manufactures Model T.	World War I begins.	Dada Movement	World War I ends.	

Three-Dimensional Pueblo Architecture

Related Areas

Art

Language Arts

Science

Social Studies

Focus

Students study architecture.

Activity

making a pueblo village

Vocabulary

space, texture, perspective, parallel, vanishing point, horizontal, vertical, two-dimensional, three-dimensional

Materials

2 half-gallon milk cartons; ruler; glue; scissors; fine-grained sand; paintbrush; light brown tempera paint; mixing bowl; waxed paper; 9" x 12" corrugated cardboard; 8 pieces of wood dowel cut into $\frac{1}{2}$" segments; greenery; clay; brown thread

Implementation

Day 1

1. Introduce students to Frank Lloyd Wright. Show examples of his work.

2. Explain to students that they are going to become architects for a pueblo village in the southwest.

3. Show slides, videos, photos, and/or posters of pueblo villages and the Native American tribe. Students are to research and discuss the family structure, community, weather, and indigenous plants and animals to the Southwest.

Day 2

1. Have students conceptualize a modern pueblo village by drawing a sketch of a pueblo village using just squares and rectangles, adding their imagination.

2. Begin making a 3-dimensional model from their drawing.

3. Cut off the top of each of the milk cartons. Cut one carton 2" shorter than the other. Clean and dry the insides of the cartons.

4. Turn the cartons so that the flat bottom is now the roof. Cut one rectangular door on each carton near the roof.

5. Glue the pueblo structure onto the cardboard.

Three-Dimensional Pueblo Architecture

Implementation *(cont.)*

Day 2   *(cont.)*

6. Cut the twigs into desired lengths to make a ladder. Glue the twigs together, then wrap the joints with thread. Glue the ladder in place by a doorway.

7. Glue the wood dowels along the top edge of a few of the pueblo walls to represent wood poles used for roof support.

8. Decorate the exterior of the pueblo as desired with artifacts and indigenous plants.

Sample Modern Pueblo Village Drawing

Extended Activities

1. Working in groups, using two-dimensional shapes, assorted paper scraps, and three-dimensional containers, arrange the objects on a large cardboard base and attach the containers using glue or tape. Decorate the sculpture by gluing on assorted paper scraps.

2. Look at pictures of city skylines at night. Discuss the shapes of a variety of buildings. Plan an original skyline using the containers collected. Paint the shapes in black and blue and display with light behind or above.

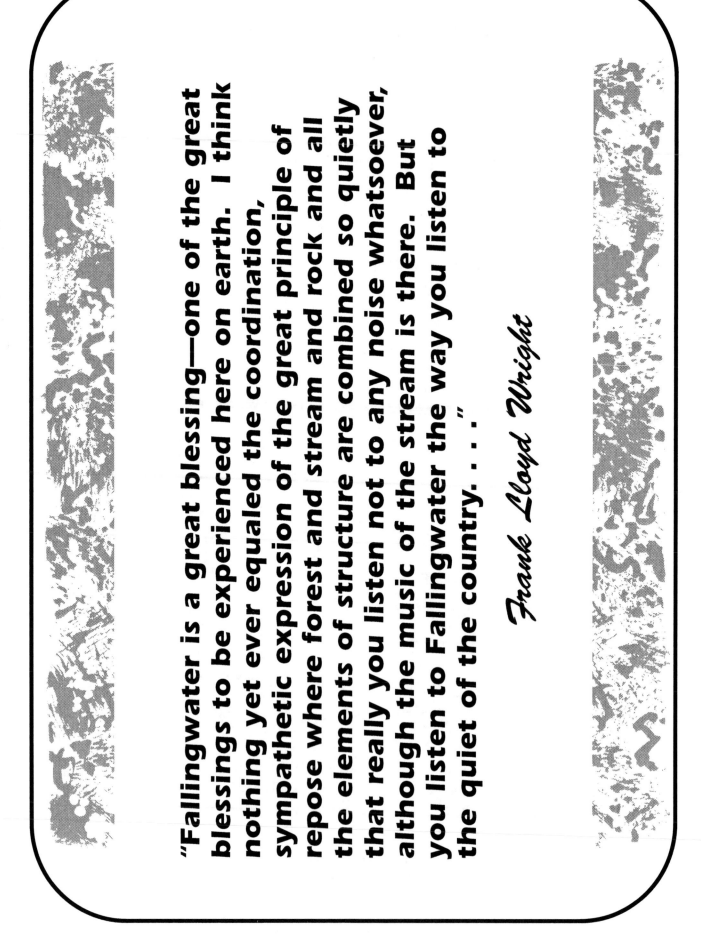

"Fallingwater is a great blessing—one of the great blessings to be experienced here on earth. I think nothing yet ever equaled the coordination, sympathetic expression of the great principle of repose where forest and stream and rock and all the elements of structure are combined so quietly that really you listen not to any noise whatsoever, although the music of the stream is there. But you listen to Fallingwater the way you listen to the quiet of the country. . . ."

Frank Lloyd Wright

1920s at a Glance

The 1920s was a decade of dramatic change. In the wake of World War I, the focus of America was inward. For the first time immigrants were not welcomed. America was changing from its pre-war, rural economy into an urban, industrial nation. Innovations and inventions flourished, changing almost every aspect of American life. Affordable automobiles changed the landscape, and radio and films brought culture and politics to everyone. Many advanced technologies, like television, computers, and space travel, have roots in the 20s.

It was a glittering time of flappers, parties, and frivolous fads. Jazz, a new and uniquely American sound, became popular. Women won the vote in time for the election of 1920. With it came a new sense of equality. They raised their hemlines, bobbed their hair, went to college, and joined the work force. Prohibition, accepted in theory, was openly flouted. Speakeasies opened by the thousands, and hip flasks were common accessories. While citizens defied the law, organized crime flourished as bootlegging became big business.

Musicians George Gershwin and Aaron Copland, writers Ernest Hemingway and F. Scott Fitzgerald, and artists Mary Cassatt and Grant Wood became prominent. In the predominantly Black populated section of Harlem in New York City, the Harlem Renaissance produced a host of great African-American writers, artists, and musicians.

On the scientific front, the 1920s was highlighted by the first radio station broadcasting over the airwaves, insulin being used for diabetes, other galaxies in the universe were discovered, and penicillin and the first color motion picture were invented. On the cultural and literary fronts, Amelia Earhart became the first woman to fly across the Atlantic, Charles Lindbergh made the first solo flight across the Atlantic, the first talking movie, *The Jazz Singer*, was exhibited, F. Scott Fitzgerald's *The Great Gatsby* was published, and the first book in the Winnie the Pooh series was published.

The stock market spiraled upward, driven by the market for durable goods and by master manipulators. Once the realm of the rich, people from all levels of society entered the market, buying on small margins. Some, like President Hoover, believed that the prosperity would last forever. But the euphoria and the decade ended on October 29, 1929, with the crash of the stock market and the dawn of the Great Depression.

Alexander Calder | **1898–1976**

Alexander "Sandy" Calder was one of the first Surrealist sculptors. Born in Lawton, Pennsylvania, Alexander always found machines fascinating. Both his father and grandfather were famous sculptors, but when it came time for Calder to choose a college, Calder chose Stephens Institute of Technology in New Jersey to major in engineering.

Upon graduating from college, Calder tried many different types of jobs in Europe and the United States. He finally returned to New York and decided to study art. He also decided that if he was going to become an artist, he was going to make it fun and exciting by constructing things which interested him.

Calder took a part time job in 1925 as a commercial artist with the *National Police Gazette.* It was during this period of his life that he began sketching people and animals at the Ringling Brothers Barnum and Bailey Circus. A year later he published his first book, *Animal Sketching* and exhibited his first show of oil paintings. Once again he traveled to Europe to study and see what other artists were doing. During his spare time, he would make wire sculptures of circus animals and people. Many of the circus figures could actually move and do things.

Calder was soon making three-dimensional figures out of wire, a hobby that he had started when he was a kid. Many of the artists who had befriended Calder thought his sculptures were fantastic and helped him get his first sculpture show in Paris. The show was a great success.

Calder decided that he wanted to try to put Mondrian's wonderful geometric shapes onto cardboard and make them come alive. He used electric motors and cranks at first but felt they were too repetitive and decided to make sculptures that floated in space naturally whenever a breeze or wind came along. Thus were born the first mobiles. Some of his mobiles were so small they would fit in your hands while others were gigantic and weighed thousands of pounds. Such is the case of the mobile that hangs in the east wing of the National Art Gallery in Washington, D.C., and weighing over 2,000 pounds.

Calder died in 1976 and is thought by many to be one of the most famous artists of the twentieth century. His art work ranges from floating mobiles and wire figures that move to kitchen utensils and toys that can be used in a home. Calder was truly a man who saw art in many forms and in many ways.

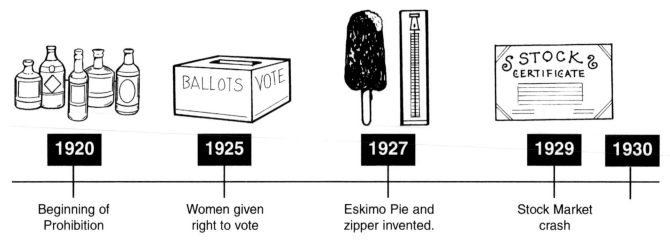

1920	1925	1927	1929	1930
Beginning of Prohibition	Women given right to vote	Eskimo Pie and zipper invented.	Stock Market crash	

Mobiles

Related Areas

Art

Language Arts

Physical Education

Science

Social Studies

Focus

Students learn that shapes can be stationary or moving (kinesthetic).

Activity

construct mobiles

Vocabulary

kinesthetic, sculpture, form, mobile, abstract, balance, primary colors, shape, space, stabiles

Materials

sheets of posterboard in primary colors (red, blue, yellow); #18–24 gauge wire; scissors; pencils; prints and poster of various kinds of mobiles; 3-D mobiles; various shaped objects for tracing (lids, cardboard shapes, stencils); 5–6 gallon size ziplock bags; color wheel; wire cutter

Implementation

Day 1

1. Go over color wheel, vocabulary, printed examples of Calder's work, and an actual 3-D mobile.

2. Students make an accordion book with vocabulary words illustrating the words.

3. Have a classroom discussion about Alexander Calder and then assign students into small groups. Instruct each group to write 3 to 5 facts it learned about the artist and be ready to have one member of each group share their ideas with the rest of the class.

4. Teacher asks each group to share an interesting fact with the rest of the class. The teacher then writes this information on chart paper. Upon completion of this task, the whole class reads the information together. Chart paper is then displayed until completion of the activity.

Day 2

1. Review yesterday's lesson.

2. Show examples of mobiles.

3. Discuss the steps needed to make a mobile while demonstrating with 2 mobiles—one out of balance and one balanced. Review the vocabulary: balance, size, shape, and space.

4. Divide the class into groups of 3–4 students. Pass out ziplock sandwich bags, containing pieces of pre-cut wire, poster board, tracing items, hole puncher, and scissors.

5. Have the students cut out various shapes and sizes from poster board. Next, have them punch a hole in each shape.

Mobiles (cont.)

Implementation (cont.)

Day 2 (cont.)

6. Students take the wire and attach each length of wire together to make their mobile.

7. Students take their cutouts and attach each piece to the wire frame of the mobile by twisting the ends of the wire to form a small loop through the poster board pieces.

8. Display the students' mobiles in the room.

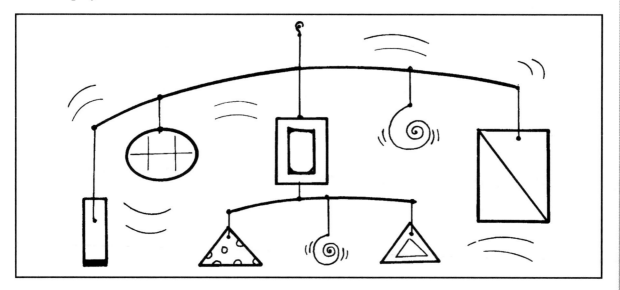

Extended Activities

1. See Calder's *Circus*. After discussion of Calder's circus characters, students divide up into groups and make their own three-dimensional circus figures out of wire. The circus figures can then be displayed in class.

2. Using natural objects from outside, (i.e., leaves, twigs, branches, shells, feathers) students make a "Celebration of Nature" mobile.

3. After a unit on the solar system, students could make a mobile using the different images of the solar system. Materials such as Styrofoam balls, wire, and construction paper, could be used to create different effects.

4. Calder was also well known for his stabiles. They often reminded people of insects, birds, and other animals. Using objects such as buttons, toothpicks, beads, feathers, shells, bolts, glue, masking tape, and other objects gathered at school and at home, students can make wonderful stabiles of their own to be displayed in the classroom. Stories about their stabiles can be written incorporating reading and writing into this activity.

5. Sandy Calder was an artist of many talents. Besides his mobiles and stabiles, he also painted as well as created toys, eating utensils, and many other kinds of objects. Give your students a variety of objects such as different sizes of wire, caps, bolts, and toothpicks. Ask them to invent some kind of kitchen utensil. Have the students make up a commercial to sell their new invention and videotape their ad.

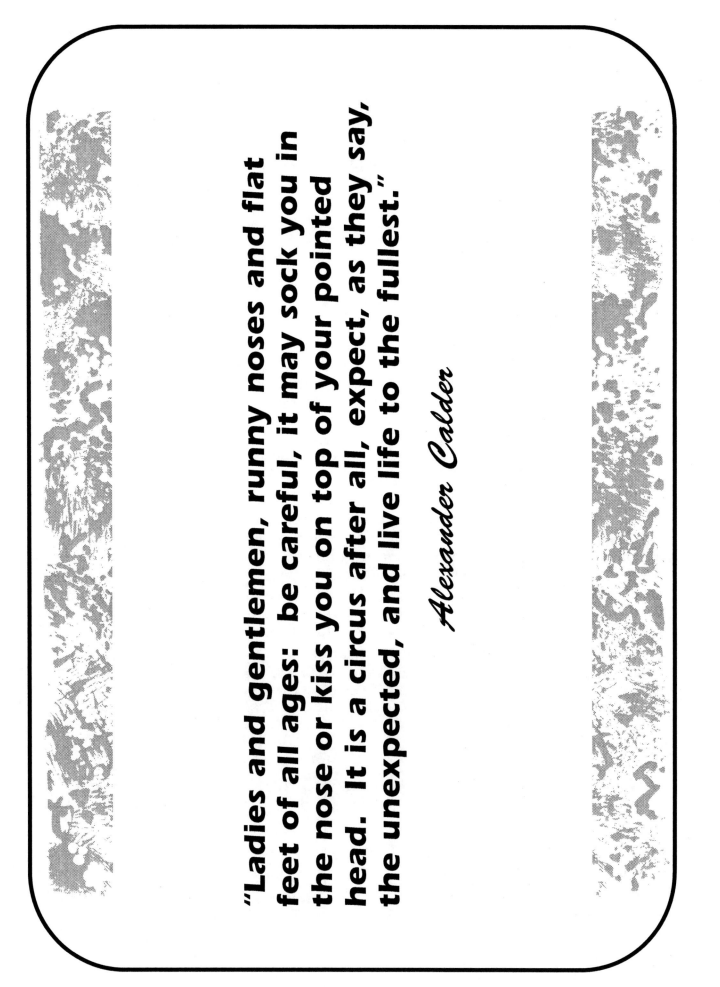

"Ladies and gentlemen, runny noses and flat feet of all ages: be careful, it may sock you in the nose or kiss you on top of your pointed head. It is a circus after all, expect, as they say, the unexpected, and live life to the fullest."

Alexander Calder

Georgia O'Keeffe   **1887–1986**

Georgia O'Keeffe has become one of the most well-known and celebrated female artists of the 20th Century. Her interpretation of the world around her gave those who viewed her paintings, a new and unique way of looking at a flower, building, or sunset. She opened up a whole new universe of bold colors and shapes that ran off the page and into your mind.

O'Keeffe was born in 1887 in Sun Prairie, Wisconsin. Even as a little girl, O'Keeffe showed an intense interest in art. Her mother, realizing O'Keeffe's passion for art, enrolled her in several different art classes. O'Keeffe loved her art classes but did not always appreciate her instructor's suggestions on how she could improve her paintings.

In 1902 the O'Keeffe family moved to Williamsburg, Virginia, where her mother enrolled her in a boarding school for girls in Chatham, Virginia. She continued her love of art at Chatham and after graduation moved to Chicago to attend the Art Institute. Although she learned to draw the human figure, it was not until she moved to New York City in 1907 that she began to learn to paint what she had visualized ever since she was a child.

With the help of her instructor, William Merritt Chase, she began to paint objects like flowers, buildings, and skylines using bold strokes. She learned to be true to herself and her paintings took on a whole new dimension. Her paints were bold and her colors exploded with energy. She began painting full time in 1918 when she moved to New York. Among her admirers was a famous photographer, Alfred Stieglitz, whom she married in 1924. Stieglitz was the only person O'Keeffe didn't mind having nearby when she was painting. They often traveled to the countryside where Stieglitz took photographs and O'Keeffe painted.

In 1929 O'Keeffe decided to visit New Mexico. She would venture out into the desert alone, often sleeping in her car, staying until she found something that interested her. Among the things that fascinated her were bones. Bones gave her a vehicle to paint the flowers and landscapes of New Mexico that she had grown to love but didn't know how to express. She painted the blue sky, the red hills, and clouds by using bones as windows. Some people laughed at her paintings of bones while others saw the beauty and wonder that O'Keeffe saw. Several successful exhibits were held in New York to show off her paintings of the Southwest where she spent her summers.

In 1946 Stieglitz died and O'Keeffe decided to move to New Mexico and make it her permanent home. O'Keeffe continued to be fascinated with the power of the mysterious desert landscape and to paint it with bold, bigger than life colors and lines until her death in 1986 at the age of 98.

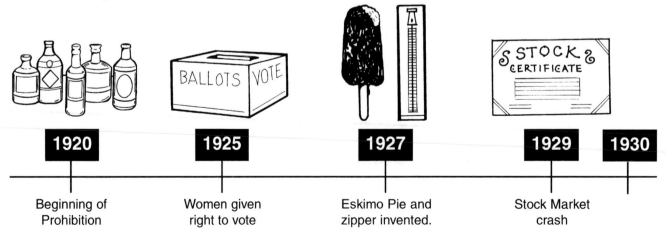

1920	**1925**	**1927**	**1929**	**1930**
Beginning of Prohibition	Women given right to vote	Eskimo Pie and zipper invented.	Stock Market crash	

Watercolor Painting

Related Areas

Art

Language Arts

Science

Social Studies

Focus

Students study the art of watercolor painting.

Activity

making a watercolor painting

Vocabulary

watercolor, sketching, microscopic view, texture, graduation, complementary colors, monochromatic colors

Materials

watercolor paper; pencils; watercolors; paintbrushes of various sizes for each student; container for water; cardboard slightly larger than paper for students to tape watercolor paper; toilet-paper rolls; salt; frames

Implementation

Day 1

1. Introduce Georgia O'Keeffe to students. Show example of her work with special emphasis on her microscopic views of plant life (and if age-appropriate, animal skulls).

2. Introduce watercolor technique by examples and demonstration.

3. Take students outside and use "microscopes" (toilet paper rolls) to select the area they are going to sketch.

4. Once students have selected their subject, have them sketch it lightly with a pencil on their white paper. Collect student papers at the end of the period.

Day 2

1. Students watch another demonstration on washing and brushing techniques. Students then practice these techniques.

2. Pass out sketches to students. Students then paint their scene with watercolors, mixing their watercolors to produce soft, monochromatic colors. (If the class hasn't had a lesson about mixing colors, the teacher should allow students to practice on paper before trying to do their painting.)

Watercolor Painting *(cont.)*

Implementation *(cont.)*

Day 2 *(cont.)*

3. Lay the finished product on newspapers to dry. (*Optional:* Sprinkle salt for a fun explosion of colors.)

4. Mount pictures on white construction paper for inexpensive frames (check out art stores for donations). Discuss the different effects of different colors. How did the toilet-paper roll help students focus on their subjects?

Extended Activities

1. Using real or fake flowers, have students do a watercolor of some flowers. Emphasize using bold strokes. Have students use large 2" sponge brushes for this activity.

2. Make a Georgia O'Keeffe museum in one part of the room or in a hallway and invite other classes to visit the museum. Have your students act as docents and discuss Georgia O'Keeffe with the visiting classes, giving them a guided tour.

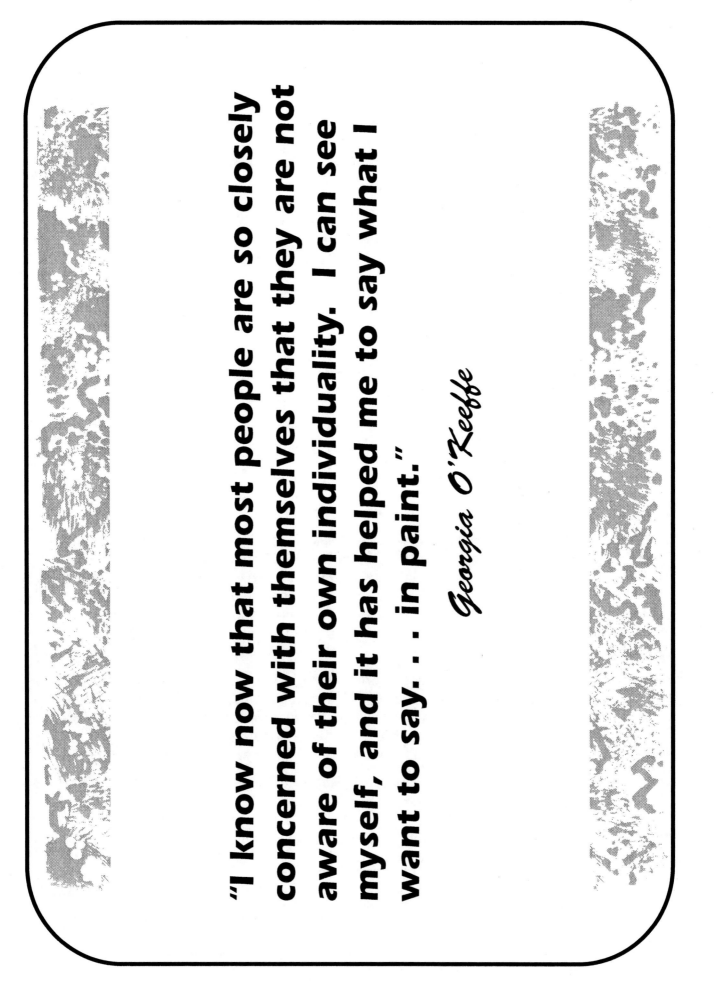

"I know now that most people are so closely concerned with themselves that they are not aware of their own individuality. I can see myself, and it has helped me to say what I want to say. . . in paint."

Georgia O'Keeffe

1930s at a Glance

The 1930s were a time of unemployment, the stock market crash, and economic disaster for millions of Americans. President Hoover left the problem to the people, and it was not until Franklin Delano Roosevelt became president in 1932 that things began to change. Roosevelt spent his first months in office providing opportunities for Americans to get back on their feet. It took several years before many Americans were able to provide a decent life for their families.

During this period in U.S. history, the invention of the radio brought entertainment, news, and music into the living rooms of millions of Americans. Similarly, the events of the war and current events of the country were being brought into the homes of Americans for the first time.

Writers, artists, and photographers were subsidized by the government to record the events in America. They recorded life in the thirties with stark realism. The Dust Bowl found many Americans living the life of immigrants. The horrid conditions that the migrant family had to endure can best be seen in Dorothea Lange's *Migrant Mother.* This photograph of a mother and her children is still haunting to anyone who sees it.

Grant Wood was also one of the artists who painted rural America. Wood was one of these realists, but he added another twist—primitivism. His most famous painting is *American Gothic*, which shows simple country folk in realistic style.

Grandma Moses is an inspiration to all who think life is over the older you become. Grandma Moses began her painting at the age of 66 when her arthritis made it difficult for her to do the needlepoint she enjoyed so much. Her son had taken her work to be displayed at a local drugstore in a town near Greenwich, New York. It sat there until an amateur collector, Louis Caldor, saw them and not only bought all of them, but went to meet her. She continued her painting until she died in 1961 at the age of 88—a true success story!

The 1930s saw many record-setting sporting events. For example, the New York Yankees won the World Series four times in succession, and Jesse Owens set five world track records in one day. Meanwhile, scientific advancements during this era included the discovery of the planet Pluto, development of the Richter Scale to measure earthquakes, and invention of the radio telescope.

On the literary front, this decade saw the publication of such famous works as John Steinbeck's Grapes of Wrath, Pearl S. Buck's *The Good Earth,* Zora Neale Hurston's *Their Eyes Were Watching God,* and Margaret Mitchell's *Gone with the Wind.* This decade also saw the completion of the Empire State Building and the Hoover Dam and the debut of Bugs Bunny and Superman.

Grant Wood   **1891–1942**

Born in 1891, Grant Wood was raised on a small Iowa farm. He loved the life of a farming family and even had his own animals that he was totally responsible for. He also loved to draw pictures of the countryside with the end of a burnt stick his mother gave him from the stove. At the age of 10, however, his father died and his family was forced to move to the city of Cedar Rapids. It was a hard transition for Wood, but eventually, his artistic talent helped him find his place as a boy of the city. He used his artistic talents to draw pictures for his high school yearbook and in designing scenery for school plays.

Upon graduation in 1910, Wood tried his hand at many things. He worked as a carpenter, decorated people's houses, made jewelry, and took art classes. In 1920 Wood decided to travel to Europe to study Impressionism. His earlier paintings show the influence of such impressionistic artists as Sisley and Pissarro, but even though his paintings were good, he still felt that he hadn't found his own style.

On a trip to Germany, Wood saw the works of some of the old master painters of the 15th century. He was immediately impressed by their paintings of everyday people depicted clearly and simply. He liked the way they carefully blended and used smooth brush strokes. Wood also liked the way the old masters took time to paint the background in detail, paying attention to the smallest detail.

Wood returned to the United States and decided to paint the thing he knew and loved best, the countryside of Iowa. His first painting was a portrait of his mother. He continued to paint rural America. He entered one of his paintings *American Gothic* in a big art show at the Art Institute of Chicago and won third place. He found himself an overnight success. Americans loved the way Wood portrayed rural America. He showed the heartland and the people who worked the land as no other artist had. He continued to paint the rural America that he loved until his death in 1942. His paintings are a wonderful legacy to the heartland of America and the people who helped build it.

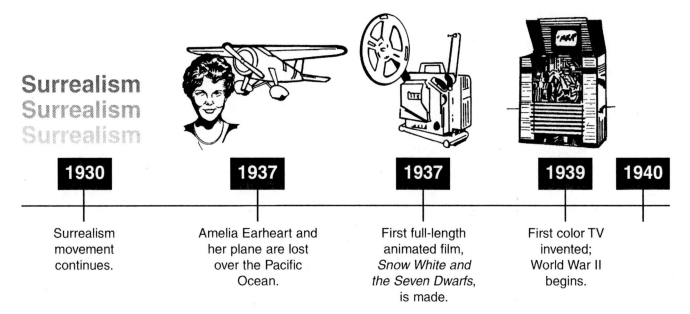

Surrealism
Surrealism
Surrealism

1930	1937	1937	1939	1940
Surrealism movement continues.	Amelia Earheart and her plane are lost over the Pacific Ocean.	First full-length animated film, *Snow White and the Seven Dwarfs*, is made.	First color TV invented; World War II begins.	

Portrait Painting

Related Areas

Art

Social Studies

Language Arts

Focus

Students will expand their skills of drawing the human face.

Activity

creating a portrait using Renaissance influence.

Vocabulary

Renaissance, negative space, profile, positive space

Materials

9" x 12" drawing paper; pencil; fine-tip, black markers; crayons

Implementation

Day 1

1. Explain that a profile is a side view of a person's face. Many profiles were painted in this style during the Renaissance era. Renaissance profiles showed well-defined contours and also used the space behind the face (the negative space) as part of the overall picture.

2. Have one student or a group of students take turns modeling and sit in a profile position.

3. Notice placement of features as they relate to each other: the corner of the eye is in line with the top of the ear and the bottom of the ear lines up with the bottom of the nose.

4. Notice that the eyes look different from the side than they do from the front. Also notice the rounded proportion of the back of the head. (Having a chart with the outline and proportions of the head would be helpful.)

Day 2

1. Start your profile sketch in pencil. You may use the models throughout the drawing or just use them for steps 2–4 to demonstrate the feature placement.

2. Add features onto your profile pencil sketch. Try to depict a well-defined (clean cut) contour. Add details for clothes and hair style.

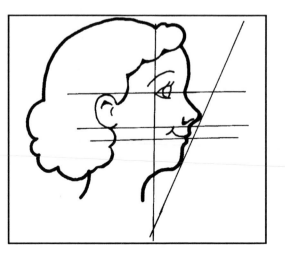

Portrait Painting *(cont.)*

Day 2   *(cont.)*

3. Create a background (a deep-space scene in the negative space): a countryside, castle, etc.

4. Color in areas, then outline with a fine-tip marker.

Extended Activities

1. Have students adjust the landscape, using the colors of the earth (browns, greens, blues). Use different mediums like colored chalk, pastel chalk, tempera paints. How does a different medium change the picture? Mood?

2. Have students draw a famous historical scene (Bunker Hill, Oregon Trail, etc.).

Extended Technology Activity

Design a magazine cover using a famous painting and photos of students in the class.

1. Find a reproduction of a famous painting.

2. Using a digital camera, take a photograph of a student in your class.

3. Save photos in *Adobe PhotoShop*.

4. Scan all images.

5. Superimpose the photographs onto the painting and into the magazine cover. Update the cover by updating the date.

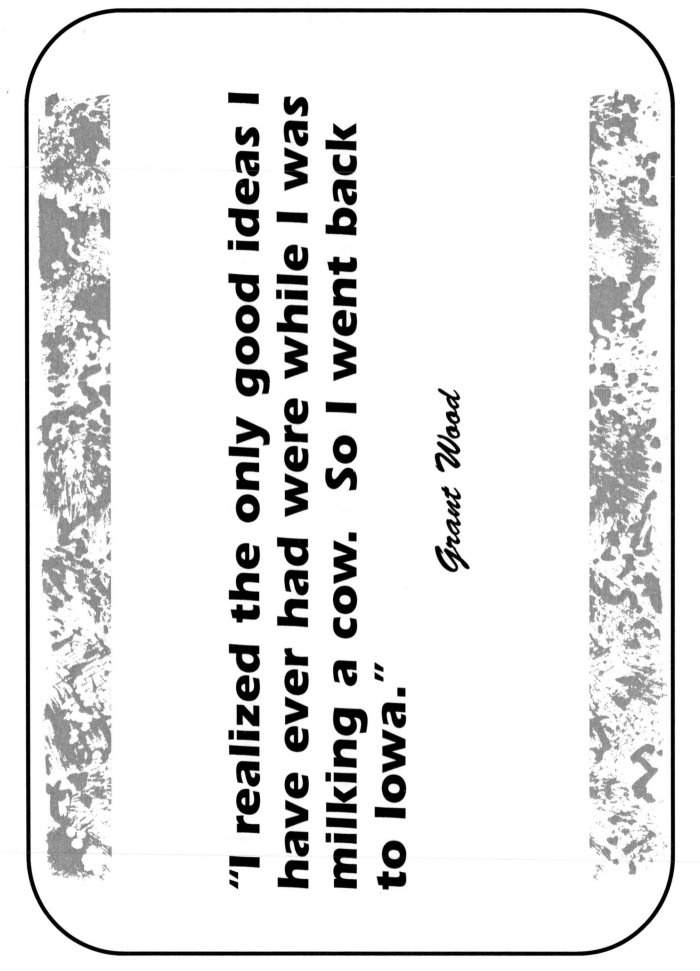

"I realized the only good ideas I have ever had were while I was milking a cow. So I went back to Iowa."

Grant Wood

Dorothea Lange

1895–1965

Dorothea Lange was an accomplished photographer who used her camera to help bring about social change during the Depression and World War II. Lange spent her early years as a photographer taking pictures of people in and around the Bay Area, becoming one of the most popular portrait photographers of the elite of San Francisco. This all changed, however, when she met Maynard Dixon, a Western artist. He introduced her to the picturesque Southwest, and she began traveling with him. Dixon would do his sketching while Lange photographed the people and landscape around her.

During a trip through the California countryside in 1929, Lange had what she referred to as "a spiritual awakening" which was to change the way she was to view photography for the rest of her life. She decided, while watching a thunderstorm, that she was going to concentrate on photographing people regardless of whether they could pay or not. This was the beginning of Lange's moving out of a studio and into an approach called "documentary photography."

Lange began photographing bread lines, labor demonstrations, and tenant farmers to show the impact of the Depression on the people in the 1930s. Her empathy towards her subjects is readily apparent in her photographs. Her now famous photograph, taken in 1936 and titled *Migrant Mother* appeared in many newspapers throughout the country. This powerful photograph of a desperate and hungry mother brought overwhelming praise to Lange as well as bringing the plight of the tenant farmers to the attention of the American people and federal government.

Lange continued photographing the effects of history on people through the thirties as well as into the forties and World War II. She worked for the Farm Securities Administration (FSA) documenting the plight of poverty stricken subjects throughout the United States. She also became well-known for her photo documentation of the Japanese internment camps. Lange's photographs not only showed their pain, but because of her great empathy for her subjects, she was able to capture their inner strength and will to survive their situation.

Throughout her long career, Lange never viewed herself as an artist. The photographs taken by Lange so many years ago, however, are living proof of how she used her cameras as an instrument for social change. Dorothea Lange's photographs will always serve as a reminder of the impact history plays on the human spirit.

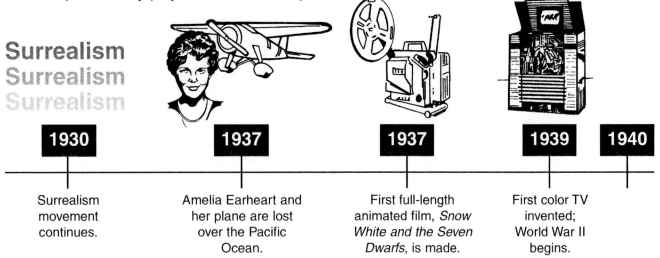

Surrealism
Surrealism
Surrealism

| 1930 | 1937 | 1937 | 1939 | 1940 |

Surrealism movement continues.

Amelia Earheart and her plane are lost over the Pacific Ocean.

First full-length animated film, *Snow White and the Seven Dwarfs*, is made.

First color TV invented; World War II begins.

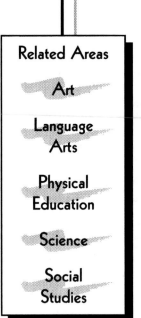

Related Areas

Art

Language Arts

Physical Education

Science

Social Studies

Documentary Photography

Focus

Students learn to use photography to tell a story.

Activity

photographing people in the school community

Vocabulary

photography, camera, photographer, artist, documentary

Materials

35 mm cameras; black and white film; old calendars and magazines with photographs of people; construction paper; twenty-five to thirty 4" x 4" square frames; chart paper; foam core board (optional)

Implementation

Day 1

Divide students into groups of 3–4 students. Each group is given one picture and five minutes to discuss and write down words that express how the pictures make them feel. After five minutes each group shows the photograph and gives the words they used to describe the picture. The teacher displays the student's photograph and writes the words on chart paper below the photograph. This process is repeated until each group has had their turn.

Days 2–3

Take students on several short field trips around their school during different school activities (i.e., P.E., recess, lunch, library period, assemblies). The amount of time for this activity depends on the flexibility of the schedule and whether parent volunteers or aides can help. Give each student a 4" x 4" frame which they will use to view their subject(s) through. Each child will use this frame to hold up to his or her eyes to view his or her subject.

Help students use this frame to really focus in on what they are really seeing. This activity will also help prepare them for taking their actual photograph.

Once back in the room, discuss how viewing through a frame allows you to focus on a subject without distractions. Light, space, and balance are also more clearly defined.

Days 4–5

Review the past 2 days' activities. Review how the frame helped focus on their subject. Explain that a camera is like a frame. It allows the photographer to focus in on the subject and choose the distance, as well as balance what you need in the photograph with what is not necessary.

Documentary Photography *(cont.)*

Implementation *(cont.)*

Days 4–5 *(cont.)*

Explain that you are going to tell the story of your school and its inhabitants through photography. Discuss the activities that you have seen over the past 2 to 3 days and have students sign up for the activity that they wish to photograph. The time allotted for this time will depend on your time frame as well as resources available to you. Have students take 1 to 3 pictures. Explain to students that they must ask permission of their subjects before they take their picture. It may be beneficial to you to let your principal know what you are doing.

Day 6

Once the photographs are developed, return photos to each student and have them each select their best photograph to be framed. Frame these photographs. Possible framing material would be black construction paper, foam board, poster board, or matting board. (Check frame stores for discounts to teachers.) Display photographs in class, local art gallery, or library, or, better yet, in a prominent place in your school.

Extended Activities

1. Have students study Ansel Adams and compare his style with Dorothea Lange. Questions for discussion: How are the two photographers alike? How are they different? Why do you think they both chose black and white over color? You could have students take photographs of nature and display them in a school gallery with Dorothea Lange's photos.

2. Have students take colored pictures of people and discuss the following: How is the mood of the colored photographs different from those done in black and white? When would colored photos be better than black and white and vice versa?

3. Have students look at black and white or colored paintings and discuss the differences and likenesses. Can a drawing or painting be just as powerful as a photograph? How? Why or why not?

4. Students can put together an album of their pictures with captions and human interest stories about their subjects. (**Note to Teachers:** This activity may require written permission from parents or staff members who appear in the photographs.)

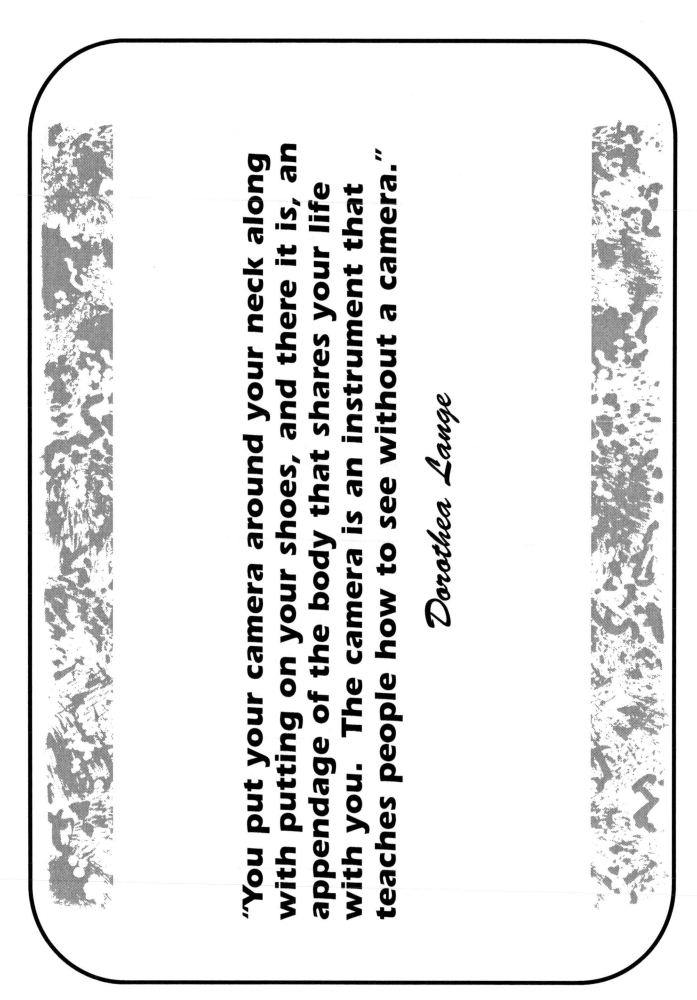

"You put your camera around your neck along with putting on your shoes, and there it is, an appendage of the body that shares your life with you. The camera is an instrument that teaches people how to see without a camera."

Dorothea Lange

1940s at a Glance

The 1940s witnessed history's first truly global war. A total of 38 countries fought on the side of the Allies against 10 Axis countries. World War I was fought in faraway Europe. In World War II, there was a very real possibility that America could be invaded. During the twenties and thirties, America held to a policy of neutrality and isolationism. In the late 1930s, the rise of totalitarian governments in Europe and their aggression toward neutral countries caused concern in America. President Roosevelt called on the nation to prepare for war and provided support for Allies in Europe and China. This wartime economy brought prosperity and an end to the Great Depression.

World War II was fought throughout different parts of Europe, Asia, and Africa. It provided an opportunity for the likes of Adolph Hitler in Germany and Benito Mussolini in Italy to gain more power and attain territorial expansion. As the war waged in different parts of the globe, America's role changed with the attack on Pearl Harbor on December 8, 1941. Subsequently, America declared war, and men were sent to battle.

On the home front, factories retooled, making tanks instead of automobiles. Women assumed new roles in society as men went off to fight, taking jobs in war plants and becoming the financial providers in their households. As months passed into years, the war effort resulted in numerous products, from food to gasoline, being rationed, as resources went to support the troops. Meanwhile, in New Mexico, scientists developed a new and terrifying weapon—the atomic bomb. Eventually, two atomic bombs would be dropped over Japan and contributed to the end of World War II.

Although the war itself and its after effects enveloped the world, there was much scientific and social/cultural progress amid all the chaos. The 1940s witnessed the completion of Mount Rushmore, the Pentagon, and the first nuclear reactor. It also witnessed the invention of the first jet fighter plane in Germany, the first electronic computer, transistor, and the Polaroid Camera too. On the literary front, the 1940s saw the publication of Ernest Hemingway's *For Whom the Bell Tolls,* Richard Wright's *Native Son, The Diary of Anne Frank,* and the first of several Curious George books.

Ultimately, it is the legacy of World War II that left the indelible impression in the 1940s. Although the fighting ended, a Cold War among the war participants followed. The United Nations, formed in 1944, helped to prevent escalation of the tensions, and America pledged to assist and protect European countries. At the end of the war, America had unleashed its atomic bomb. Russia began an arms race and developed its own atomic bomb in 1949.

Walt Disney   **1901–1966**

Walt Disney was born in 1901 in Chicago, Illinois. His family later moved to Marceline, Missouri. Growing up on a farm, Walt was surrounded by animals of which he loved to sketch. As a child he became interested in drawing, selling his drawings to friends and relatives when he was only seven years old. In high school Disney enjoyed drawing and photography. He worked on his high school paper and attended the Academy of Fine Arts in Chicago at night.

Walt tried joining the military at 16 but was turned down. He then joined the Red Cross and was sent to Europe where he worked as an ambulance driver. His ambulance was covered with cartoon characters.

In 1923 Walt decided to join his brother Roy in Hollywood, California. They pooled what money they had, borrowed $250 from an uncle, and set up a shop in their uncle's garage. Walt and his brother wanted to do cartooning. Walt had already completed an animated fairy tale. Their first order was from a New York firm that wanted them to produce *Alice in Cartoonland.* Their business began to grow slowly but steadily. In 1928 Walt created Mickey Mouse in the world's first sound cartoon called *Steamboat Willie.*

During a 43-year Hollywood career, Disney became a pioneer in cartooning, television, animation, and movies for children. *Snow White, Cinderella,* and *Bambi,* are just three of his cartoon features that have thrilled children and adults across the globe. Television opened up a whole new world for Disney. He started with the *Mouseketeer Club* in the 1950s and *Wonderful World of Color* in 1961.

Nobody knows for sure when the idea of Disneyland came to Disney, but as soon as the idea began, he started putting a plan into action. What started out to be a two-acre amusement park turned into a bigger-than-life "Magic Kingdom" with rides, rivers, underground caves, as well as many of the Disney cartoon characters that everyone loved so much. In 1955 Disneyland opened to the world. It contained 165 acres of a magical world that has been enjoyed by millions every day of the year.

In 1964 President Lyndon B. Johnson awarded Walt Disney the Presidential Medal of Freedom, the highest decoration the United States government can bestow upon a civilian. It is an honor fitting for a man whose name represents imagination, optimism, and vision. Through his work he brought joy, happiness, and magic to children as well as adults all over the world. He showed that creating the impossible was possible.

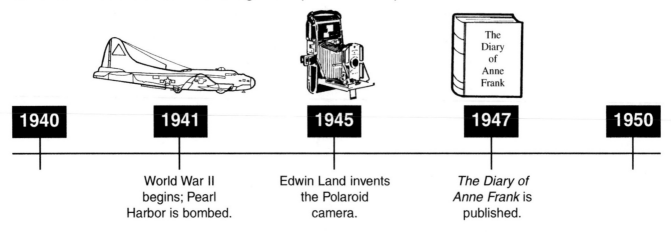

1940	**1941**	**1945**	**1947**	**1950**
	World War II begins; Pearl Harbor is bombed.	Edwin Land invents the Polaroid camera.	*The Diary of Anne Frank* is published.	

Drawing a Cartoon

Related Areas

Art

Language
Arts

Focus

Students become aware of the cartooning perspective and the advancement of cartooning from the 1930s to the present by studying the works of Walt Disney and the Walt Disney Studios.

Activity

drawing a cartoon character and creating a cell

Vocabulary

cartoon, cell, character, film, transparency, animation

Materials

a video of some Walt Disney characters; poster examples of their works; comic books; cartoon example; acrylic paint; transparency film; white paper; pencils; permanent black markers; tempera paint; watercolor paint

Implementation

Day 1

1. Hand out paper and permanent, black, felt-tip markers.

2. Using a pencil, each student draws a carton character at least half the size of an 8.5" x 11" sheet of white paper.

3. When the cartoon character is accepted by the teacher, each student traces the image onto a sheet of film, using a black permanent marker.

Day 2

1. Paint the character on the back side of the film, using flat tempera colors, staying within or on the black lines. Let dry over night.

Day 3

1. On a sheet of white paper, draw a landscape that goes with the cartoon character in the background, using one-point perspective.

Drawing a Cartoon *(cont.)*

Sample Cartoon Drawing

Extended Activity

Cartoon Strip

1. Student uses his or her cartoon character with a story line in a 5-square storyboard.

2. Using one point perspective, draw a background and repeat it in each square.

Extended Technology Activity

1. Animate the cartoon character using animation software such as *KidPix* or *HyperCard*.

2. Make a short animation movie or computer slide show presentation.

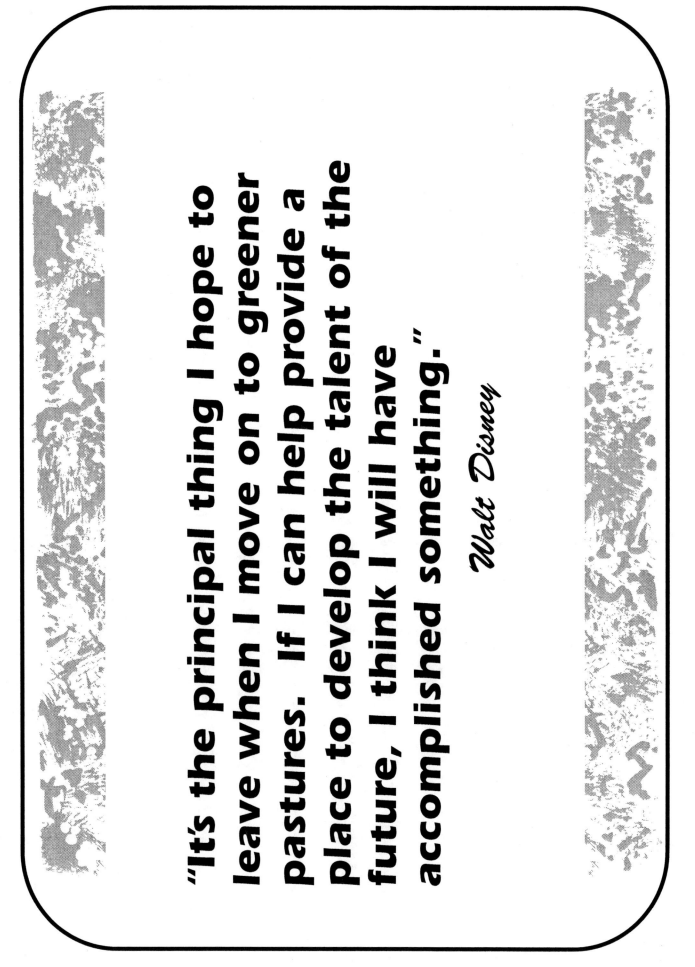

"It's the principal thing I hope to leave when I move on on to greener pastures. If I can help provide a place to develop the talent of the future, I think I will have accomplished something."

Walt Disney

Norman Rockwell   1894–1978

Norman Rockwell was born in New York City in 1894. He knew from an early age that he wanted to be an artist. Rockwell attended both the New York School of Art and the National Academy of Design while still in his teens. He would later transfer to the Art Students League to study with Thomas Fogarty and George Bridgman. It was Fogarty's instruction in illustration that prepared Rockwell for his first commercial commissions. Bridgman taught Rockwell the technical skills that he relied on throughout his career.

Rockwell's career, like his love for art, began at an early age. At the age of 15, he was commissioned to do a series of four Christmas cards. He was also working as director of Boys' Life and doing freelance work while under the age of 20. Rockwell painted his first cover for *The Saturday Evening Post* at the age of 22. He completed over 300 covers for *The Saturday Evening Post* over the next 47 years.

Rockwell's love of small-town-America is reflected in most of his paintings. He moved his family to Vermont in 1939 where he used his family, friends, and neighbors as subjects for his paintings. Some of his "subjects" are still alive and enjoy telling visitors about his museum in Stockbridge and about how they became part of a Norman Rockwell painting.

President Franklin Delano Roosevelt's address to Congress in 1943 inspired Rockwell to paint the Four Freedoms paintings for the *Saturday Evening Post*. Rockwell's interpretations of Freedom of Speech, Freedom of Worship, Freedom from Want, and Freedom from Fear were accompanied by essays by well-known writers and became enormously popular. The painter toured the United States, helping to sell millions of dollars in war bonds for the war effort.

After his 47-year association with *The Saturday Evening Post,* Rockwell worked for *Look* magazine. During his 10 years with *Look*, Rockwell painted pictures that showed his concern and interest in civil rights, poverty, and America's exploration in space.

With his health failing, he arranged to have his studio and contents added to a trust in 1976. In 1977 Rockwell received the Presidential Medal of Freedom for his "vivid and affectionate portraits of our country." He died in Stockbridge on November 8, 1978, at the age of 84. His portraits, however, live on as a testament to his love for his country.

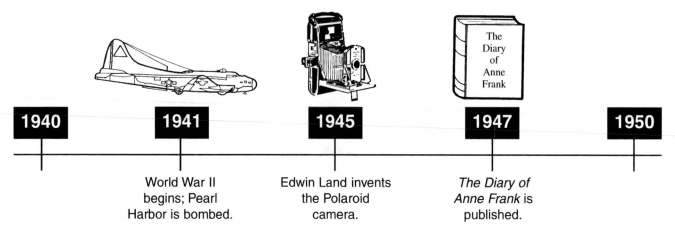

1940	1941	1945	1947	1950
	World War II begins; Pearl Harbor is bombed.	Edwin Land invents the Polaroid camera.	*The Diary of Anne Frank* is published.	

Poster Art

Related Areas

Art

Language Arts

Science

Social Studies

Focus

Students design artwork by illustrating magazine covers.

Activity

Design a poster using a topic word and illustration. Use a typeface that enhances the illustration.

Vocabulary

poster, design, font, typeface, illustration, layout, graphics, headings, subheadings

Materials

a video of the life of Norman Rockwell; poster examples of Rockwell's work; *Busy Teacher's Guide Art Lessons* from Teacher Created Resources; construction paper; cardboard lids; acrylic paint; sponge brushes; scissors; paper; pencils; old magazines; a book or chart of various typestyles

Implementation

Days 1 and 2

1. Show video about Norman Rockwell and discuss his illustrations. Hold a discussion about his life and discuss the type of illustrations that he created. Discuss the words *theme* or *topic*.

2. Choose one of Rockwell's prints. Have students discuss what they think is happening in the picture. What makes them think this?

3. Have each students select one of Rockwell's illustrations and write a story to accompany the illustration.

4. Have students share their stories with the class.

5. Display the stories in the class.

Days 3–6

1. Pass out covers from various magazines to discuss how illustrators designed the cover. How did the illustrator get his or her message across? What is the ratio of words to illustrations? Have students suggest situations or events that might make an interesting topic for a cover of a magazine.

2. Pick an actual magazine from discarded or old magazines from the school library (e.g., *Time, Newsweek,* etc.).

Poster Art *(cont.)*

3. Have students design and illustrate their own magazine covers.

4. Students use a computer to design the words or phrases for their cover. Encourage students to try different fonts and sizes for headings and subheadings. Display covers on a bulletin board.

Extended Activity

Explore how a change of font, style, or size can change the mood and/or meaning of one word or phrase.

1. Divide the class into 6 groups and hand out to each group one word or phrase.

2. Have students use the computer to experiment typing the same headline using different fonts, styles, and sizes.

3. Display by cutting out headlines and gluing them onto construction paper.

4. Select a student from each group to facilitate a classroom discussion on the mood changes and meanings found from his or her group's word or phrase.

5. Option: Add a different magazine photo for each example to see the change of mood or meaning.

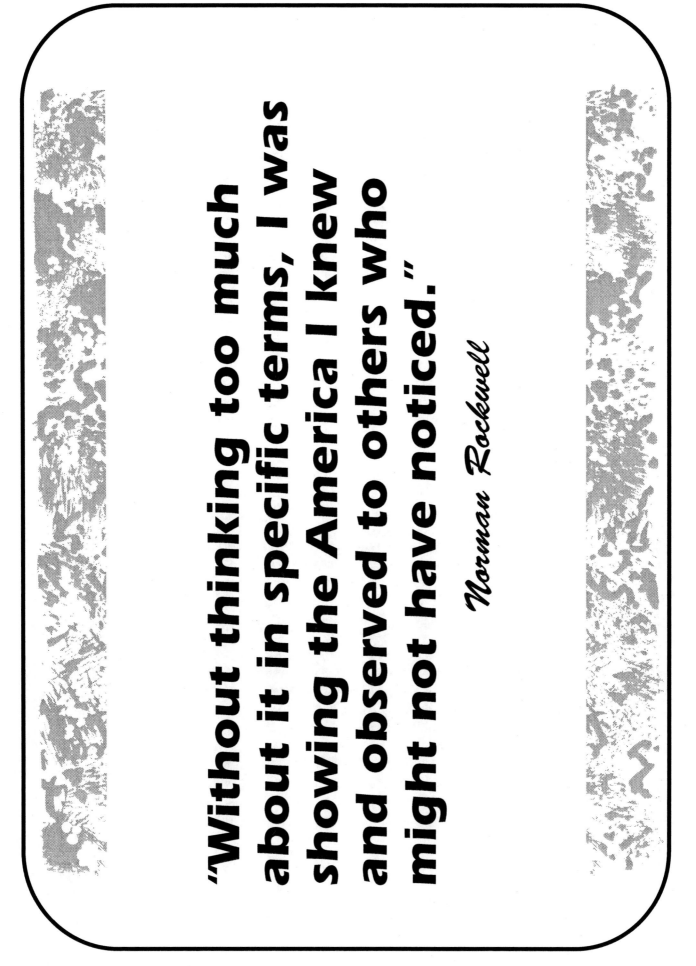

"Without thinking too much about it in specific terms, I was showing the America I knew and observed to others who might not have noticed."

Norman Rockwell

1950s at a Glance

The fifties were a time of renewal following World War II. Although the conflict in the Pacific and Europe was at an end, North Korea forces invaded South Korea and many Americans were sent to protect freedom. The fighting lasted for a period of three years. Americans were finally able to focus on their own lives and families. With the end of World War II and the Korean War, a population explosion was taking place. This "explosion" brought about more families, and more families meant there was a need for more homes. Many servicemen were taking advantage of the G.I. Bill which allowed them to purchase a home with low financing. Many families were also moving into subdivisions or suburbia.

Most women still stayed at home raising their families. A few women, however, were finding the outside job market a place to try their own wings as well as add to the family income. Margaret Chase Smith became the first woman to serve in the Senate and House of Representatives. Rosalyn Yalow and Chen-Shuing Wu became important physicists. Both women won Noble Prizes for their outstanding work in the area of science.

Science and technology saw the invention of the television which would soon change the lifestyles of the American family forever. *I Love Lucy, Gunsmoke,* and *Leave It to Beaver* were watched by millions of families every week.

Music of the 1950s was changed dramatically with the introduction of a country boy named Elvis Presley. Elvis Presley became an idol, an icon, and a legend with such songs as "Jail House Rock," "Blue Suede Shoes," and "Hound Dog." Elvis became known as the King of Rock and Roll and his music was played by young and old alike. Others like Chuck Berry, Little Richard, and Jerry Lee Lewis followed in the footsteps of Elvis.

Jasper Johns and Frank Lloyd Wright led the changes in art. Jasper Johns introduced the world to pop art, while Frank Lloyd Wright used innovative and different architectural styles. Cathedral ceilings, built-in furniture, fireplaces, and carports were some of the features that Wright changed.

Building homes using the surrounding environment was Frank Lloyd Wright's trademark. If a home was to be built in an already existing environment of trees and waterfalls, Wright incorporated those elements inside as well as outside of the home. Frank Lloyd Wright's goal was to be the greatest architect who had yet lived. His work is a testament to this idea.

Louise Nevelson   **1899–1988**

Louise Nevelson was a pioneer creator of large-wall, environmental wooden sculpture. Born in Kiev, Russia, in 1889, Louise moved to Maine with her family when she was nine years old. She always enjoyed the arts and knew at an early age that she wanted to be a sculptor. Her father worked in the lumber industry, so she had plenty of wood available to experiment with in regards to sculpture. Although she grew up working in the art of sculpturing, it was not until she was in her sixties that she was able to earn a living at it. Before this time, she was helped by her family and even sold heirlooms to support herself.

Nevelson was interested in many of the art forms and became a successful actress and dancer in her thirties and forties. Her true vocation, however, was a sculptor. She went to Germany in the 1930s and studied under a German sculptor named Hans Hofmann. She also assisted Diego Rivera. During this time, she was continually perfecting her own sculptures and ceramics.

Louise's sculptures often looked like she had taken a large box and displayed different pieces of wood and metal into unusual shapes and forms. Louise felt that art should allow the observers to form their own opinions of what the art represented to them. She did not want to form a sculpture based on rules made by others, but chose, instead, to go down her own path using her own sense of style.

Her investigations into the simplicity of form and movement in the early 1930s made her drawings of figures seem symbolic rather than representative of a male or female figure. This may be in part due to her appreciation of the work of a friend named Matisse. Her figure drawings and ceramic works of the 1930s have the same simplification of the human form with neutral spaces and exaggerated textures.

Nevelson is most known for her wall sculptures, which can be seen all over America in office buildings as well as museums. She used mainly wood as her medium and sometimes interjected steel and other metals. Nevelson worked up until her death in 1988. Throughout her life, Nevelson remained true to herself and to her art. Those who view her art, whether in a museum or in an office building, can appreciate her flare for the abstract as well as use their own imagination to create their own images and visions of what they see.

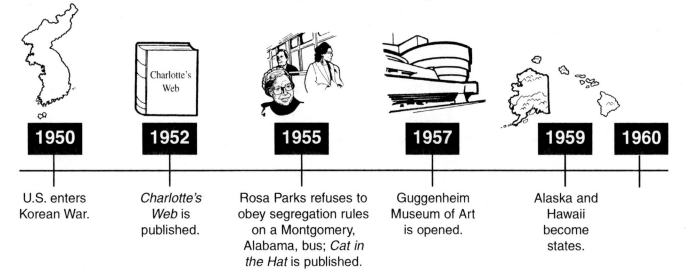

1950	1952	1955	1957	1959	1960
U.S. enters Korean War.	*Charlotte's Web* is published.	Rosa Parks refuses to obey segregation rules on a Montgomery, Alabama, bus; *Cat in the Hat* is published.	Guggenheim Museum of Art is opened.	Alaska and Hawaii become states.	

Wood Sculpture

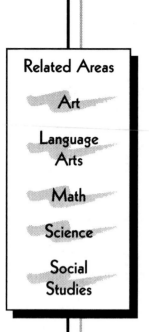
Focus

Students become aware of sculpting from their environment.

Activity

constructing a sculpture from pieces of wood scraps

Vocabulary

sculptor, sculpture, environment, metal, composition, values, collection

Materials

a video about Louise Nevelson; poster examples of her work; cardboard lids; acrylic paint; sponge brushes; scissors; paper; pencils; glue (wood glue works best); wood scraps; wood items

Implementation

1. Show a video about Louise Nevelson and discuss her compositions.

2. Divide the class into groups and assign each group a color.

3. Each group receives a large lid of a cardboard box.

4. Each group selects objects to make their sculptor.

5. With supervision from the teacher, each group paints outside of the box with paint and then lets it dry.

6. Each group paints objects to be used in the box and set on newspaper to dry.

7. Students then glue objects to their boxes.

8. Students paint the floor of their boxes and set them aside to dry.

9. After all boxes are complete, stack them on top of each other to create a Louise Nevelson-like piece. (You may need to staple them to a bulletin board to keep pieces from falling down.)

10. Then turn off the lights and have students view the boxes with flashlights to demonstrate how shadows affect and change the work.

Wood Sculpture *(cont.)*

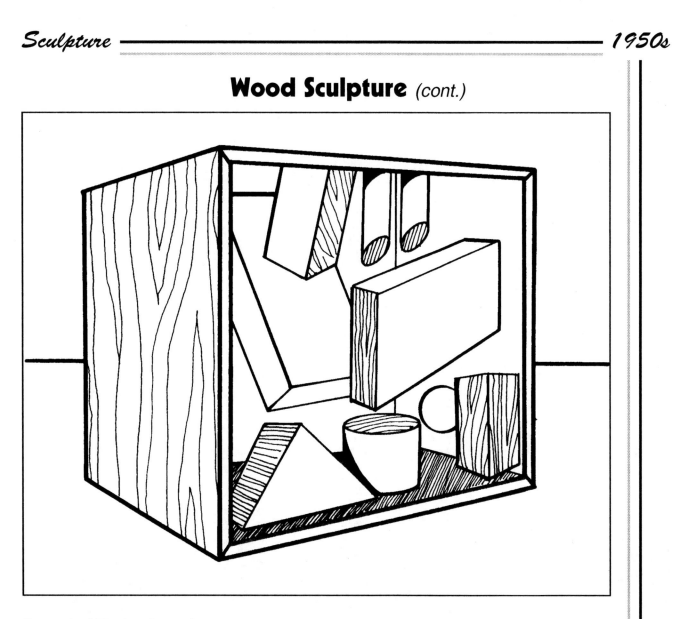

Extended Technology Activity

1. Students make a historical box with items found on the Internet, magazines, and photos from home. (Students can use a graphics software such as *Adobe Photoshop*.)

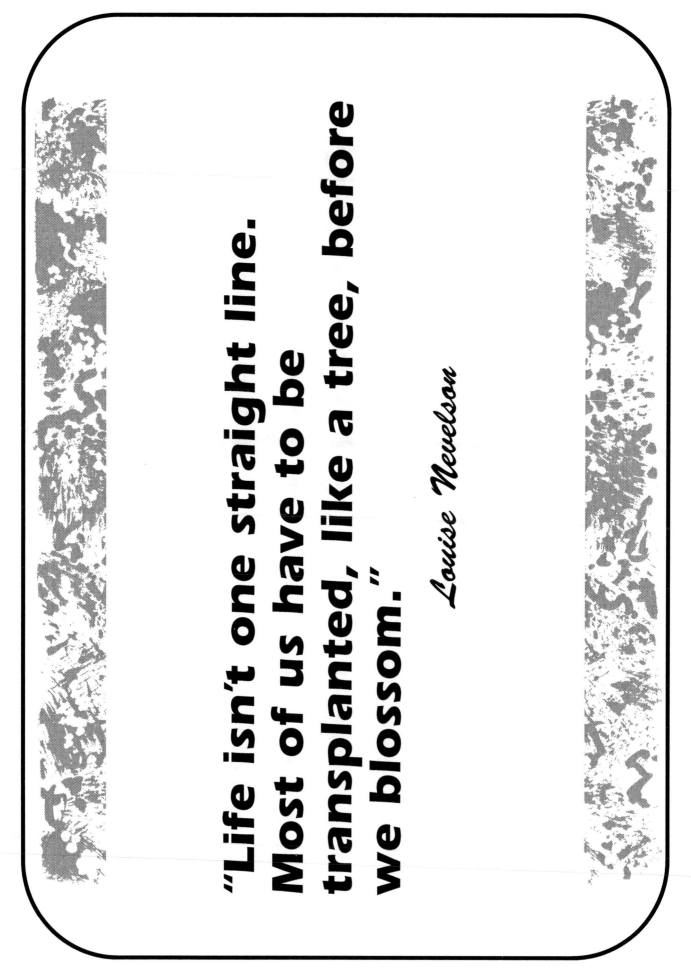

"Life isn't one straight line. Most of us have to be transplanted, like a tree, before we blossom."

Louise Nevelson

Jackson Pollock   **1912–1956**

Jackson Pollock was the first "expressionist all-over" painter, pouring paint instead of using brushes and a palette, and abandoning all conventions of realism. He danced all over his canvases spread across the floor, lost in his patternings, dripping and dribbling with total control. He felt the painting has a life of its own, and he would let it come through.

Pollock was born in 1912 in Cody, Wyoming, but his family moved that same year to Arizona and later to California. He grew up during the Great Depression in Los Angeles and began developing an interest in art at an early age. He liked the art movement known as Surrealism and at the age of 18 moved to New York City to live with his brother and go to school at the Art Students League. His teacher, Thomas Hart Benton, taught him to do landscapes and he was able to use his talent to support himself as an easel painter during the Great Depression. He had his first one-man show in 1943 at the Guggenheim's Art-of-This-Century Gallery in New York City. He was fortunate to have exhibits of his art almost every year from then on.

Jackson Pollock tried many different styles of art but found abstract art to be what he could most identify with. He was greatly influenced by the abstract painters Pablo Picasso and Joan Miro. He also liked the dreamlike and unreal aspect of the Surrealists. He used their influences to help him discover his own technique and style.

In the 1940s, Pollock tried painting what he called "action painting," a type of painting that involved using his whole body. He would place a piece of canvas on the ground and run around as fast as he could, pouring different colors of paint onto the canvas. He would sometimes fling paint onto his canvas to give it a spattered effect. He found this form of innovative painting gave him the ability to express his feelings on canvas through random patterns and shapes. He could use a variety of shape, line, and color through his "action painting." He often said that his painting controlled him and that when he was involved in his painting, he was totally unaware of what he was doing or what was happening around him. He felt that abstract painting took on a life of its own, unlike realism, which had a certain set of standards that realist painters went by. Although he died in 1956 at the age of 44, he has left a legacy of art behind him. Looking at his art, one can still feel the energy of the painting as if the canvas was still in progress, and the artist had just stepped out for a minute.

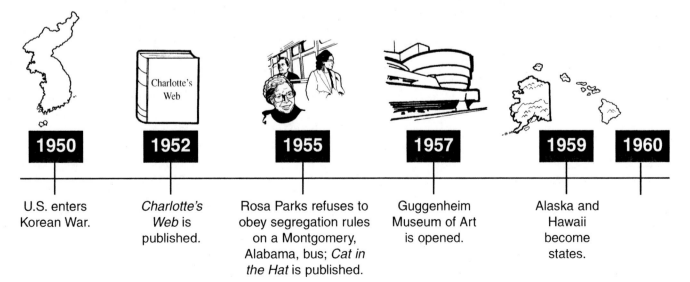

1950	**1952**	**1955**	**1957**	**1959**	**1960**
U.S. enters Korean War.	*Charlotte's Web* is published.	Rosa Parks refuses to obey segregation rules on a Montgomery, Alabama, bus; *Cat in the Hat* is published.	Guggenheim Museum of Art is opened.	Alaska and Hawaii become states.	

Action Painting

Focus

Students learn that some paintings are different from photography through the action of the artist.

Activity

create an "action painting"

Vocabulary

movement, abstract, experimentation, spatter, action painting

Materials

newspaper-covered work area or outside grassy area; smocks, old clothes, or coveralls; variety of large brushes; large containers of tempera paint; butcher paper or large sheet of craft paper

Implementation

1. Cover the work area with lots of newspaper or use a grassy area outside.

2. Cover the artist with old clothing or coveralls to prevent student from ruining good clothes.

3. Begin by having the student dip one of the brushes into a container of paint.

4. Student takes the brush loaded with color and walks around piece of paper spattering it with paint. (No more than 4 students at a time.)

5. After each student has had a turn, discuss what, if anything needs to be added to the painting.

6. Add more colors and more spattering as painting dictates.

7. Leave it outside with rocks or books to hold it down until painting is dried.

8. Display it in the classroom. Use it as a bulletin board to display individual Pollock "action paintings."

Action Painting *(cont.)*

Extended Activities

1. Students can do "action paintings" to be used as wrapping paper.

2. Have students divide up into groups. Have one group use only bold colors on their painting. Have another group use only pastel colors. How do colors change the mood of the picture?

3. Have students listen to different kinds of music and do an "action painting." How does music change the choice of colors or the way we spatter paint? Is there a difference? Why or why not?

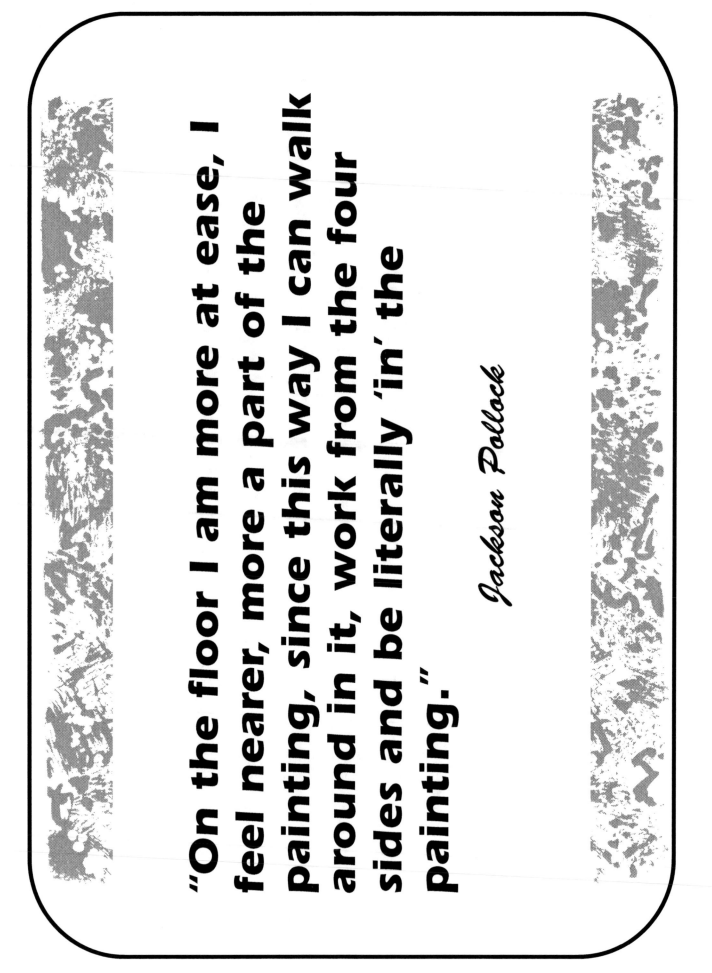

"On the floor I am more at ease, I feel nearer, more a part of the painting, since this way I can walk around in it, work from the four sides and be literally 'in' the painting."

Jackson Pollock

1960s at a Glance

It was a time of change and unrest in America. The Vietnam War was still going on. Civil Rights was still an issue that needed to be enforced rather than a right of every citizen. John F. Kennedy was the youngest president to take office. His energy and concern for the rights of every American was inspiring many young adults to join the Peace Corps, become active in the Civil Rights movement, or show their concern through song and protest marches. The assassination of John F. Kennedy, Robert Kennedy, and Martin Luther King Jr. shocked the nation and further emphasized the need for change.

The arts reflected the radical changes in America. The Beatles brought their "beat" to America and were an instant success. Folk singers like Joan Baez, Bob Dylan, and Phil Ochs sang about human rights and the injustices towards each other. Andy Warhol introduced the world of art to a new form called Pop Art. Pop Art was used to show visual images from mass culture in a modified form. Andy Warhol used vivid colors and clever designs to make the "ordinary" seem "un-ordinary." Campbell Soup cans became art on canvas. Icons such as Elvis Presley and Marilyn Monroe were made to appear larger than life; exactly the statement Andy Warhol was trying to make. *Peanuts and the Gang* became popular comic strip characters created by Charles Schultz, and *Where the Wild Things Are* became a popular children's book by author and illustrator, Maurice Sendak.

Science was also taking a giant step into space with Neil Armstrong becoming the first person to walk on the moon. With this historical walk, a new importance was being given to science and heroes were now being associated with men like Neil Armstrong and Buzz Aldrin.

Women were beginning to receive recognition for their contributions to our nation. Shirley Chisholm became the first African-American woman to be elected to the House of Representatives. Wilma Rudolph won a gold medal in the 1960 Olympics, and Billie Jean King became a champion tennis player.

The sixties were a time of change, loss, and rebirth. The changes were many, the losses heartfelt, and the rebirth of commitment an ongoing challenge to the present and future generations of America.

Andy Warhol

1928–1987

Artist, filmmaker, painter, collector, and commercial designer, Andy Warhol was all of these and more! It is no wonder that he was one of the most influential American artists of the 20th century. Andy showed great promise even as a little boy, and although Warhol's family had very little money, they managed to send him to art college.

After college, he began working for a magazine where he was asked to draw an ad for shoes. He did such a great job that he went on to do a whole series of ads for a big shoe store in New York City.

Andy was soon receiving more work than he could handle and had to hire friends and family to help him complete all the projects he had going. Besides ads, Warhol began designing greeting cards, record albums, wallpaper, and book covers. He was quickly becoming one of the wealthiest illustrators in New York City.

In the early 1960s, a new form of art was developing known as "Pop Art." Pop Art artists used commercial images from everyday life in their sculptures and paintings. Andy Warhol was greatly impressed with this new art form. He especially liked the work of Jasper Johns and Robert Rauschenberg and decided to try his hand at Pop Art.

He began exhibiting his paintings with silk screened "Pop" imagery in 1962 and moved onto painting things that people used in everyday life. One of his most famous paintings is the painting titled *Campbell's Soup*, a larger than life painting of a Campbell's Soup can.

Warhol also thought that repeated images were an important part of Pop Art because things are repeated in everyday life all the time. He painted several paintings, repeating the pattern again and again as can be seen in his paintings *One Hundred Soup Cans* and *Front and Back Dollar Bills*.

Andy's paintings became very popular. He began to print his paintings using a silk-screening method so that he could reproduce his paintings in large quantities. From here he moved on to painting and printing all kinds of popular subjects like *Shot Red Marilyn* and *Elvis I and II*.

Andy Warhol's art is an important part of our history. He made many people take a look at the world around them and see what was real and what was make believe.

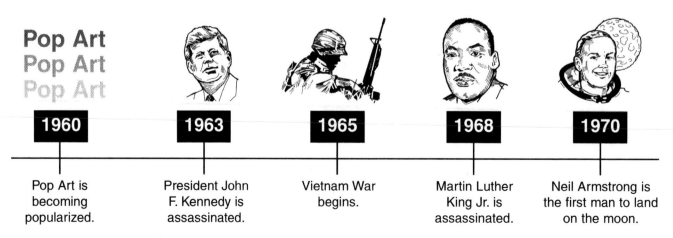

Pop Art
Pop Art
Pop Art

1960	1963	1965	1968	1970
Pop Art is becoming popularized.	President John F. Kennedy is assassinated.	Vietnam War begins.	Martin Luther King Jr. is assassinated.	Neil Armstrong is the first man to land on the moon.

Contour Drawing

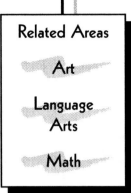
Objective

Students will learn that there is art in everyday objects.

Activity

Students will draw and decorate a shoe.

Vocabulary

Pop Art, sculpture, figurative, advertisement, realistic art, contour

Materials

a variety of shoes; 12" x 18" white butcher paper; manila and/or recycled paper; pencil; eraser; crayons; tempera paint; brushes; newsprint; examples of Andy Warhol's art

Implementation

Day 1

1. Groups of students will read about Andy Warhol in a read around activity. Allow about 15 minutes. The teacher then facilitates a discussion of life and works of Andy Warhol. Vocabulary words are reviewed with each group with a special emphasis on the word "contour."

2. Show pictures of at least 2–4 of Warhol's art. Discuss why his work was called "Pop Art."

Day 2

1. Have students take off one of their shoes. Have several different kinds of shoes available for students who feel uncomfortable taking their shoe off. (Yard sales or secondhand stores are a good source.) Students place the shoe in front of them.

2. Discuss shoe proportion.

   a. How large is the opening where the foot goes in compared to the rest of the shoe?

   b. Notice details of the shoe.

3. Pass out practice sheets of paper to each student. Students will set the shoe at the top of their desk paying close attention to details.

4. Each paper is placed horizontally or vertically if it is a boot or tall shoe.

5. Students draw with pencils, no erasers, the outline (contour) of the shoe without looking at the paper. Emphasize to the students that they need to take their time in drawing the shoe.

Contour Drawing *(cont.)*

Implementation *(cont.)*

Day 3

1. Review Day 2 lesson.
2. Teacher places Day 2 details on a chart or overhead for easy viewing for the student.
3. Explain to the students that they are going to draw a shoe again. They are to start at one point, stop and look, start again, and stop and look, and so on until drawing is completed.
4. When drawing is completed, the student is to outline their drawing with black crayon and then do a wash using tempera paint. Decorating the shoe with glitter, fabric paint, sequins, etc., is optional.
5. When their shoe art is dry, they are to cut it out and mount it onto a contrasting piece of construction paper. This activity makes a great bulletin board project. A teacher can extend this activity by having students write a poem about their shoe or write a short story about where they found this shoe.

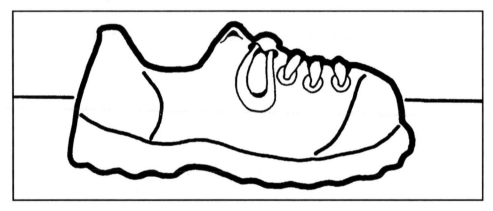

Extended Activities

1. Have students make a 3-D replica of a household item (i.e., toothpaste tube, soup can, cereal box, bun package) using boxes of many sizes and shapes (cylinders, squares, rectangles). Have the students tape their boxes together and/or bend, cut and tape oaktag to make the shape of the object. Using starch and strips of newspaper, students cover their project with a layer of newspaper that has been dipped in the starch. Use three layers and then allow project to dry. Students then paint their 3-D object with tempera paint to make it look real.
2. Students can write an ad for their 3-D replica and present it to class orally or as a video project.
3. Students can make a fast food feast by using such materials as foam, cardboard, fabric, pom-poms, glitter, panty hose, and glue. A piece of cherry pie can be made by using cardboard for the crust, foam covered with red fabric and pom-poms for the middle, and a sprinkle of red glitter on top to look like cinnamon. Pizza, pie, ice cream cones, hot dogs, hamburgers, etc., can be made with a few craft items and a lot of imagination.

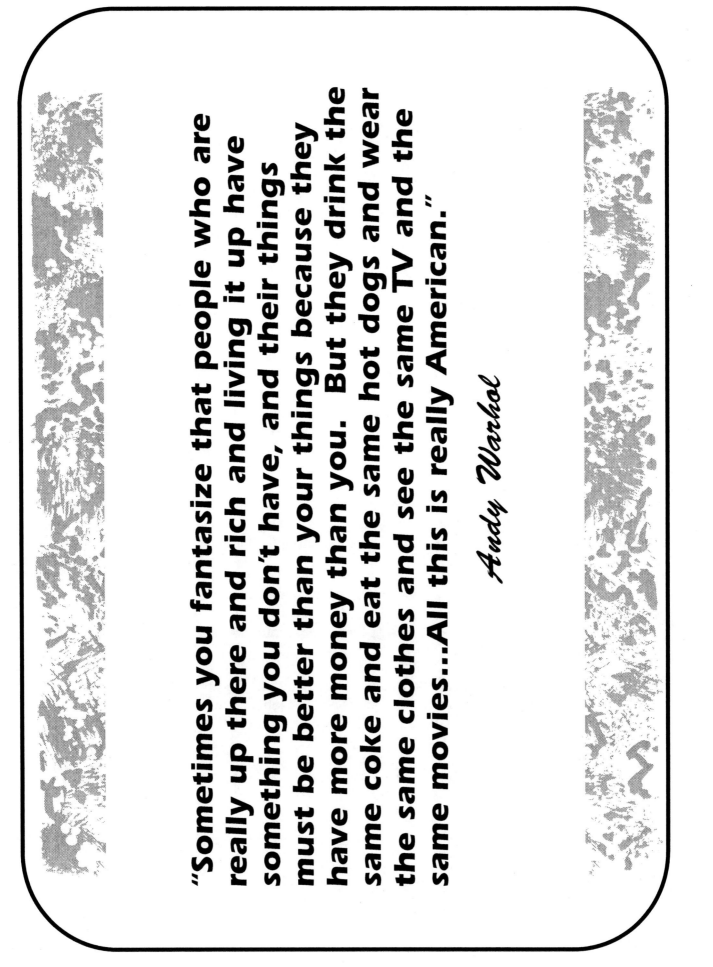

"Sometimes you fantasize that people who are really up there and rich and living it up have something you don't have, and their things must be better than your things because they have more money than you. But they drink the same coke and eat the same hot dogs and wear the same clothes and see the same TV and the same movies...All this is really American."

Andy Warhol

Judy Chicago   Born 1939–

Judy Chicago is an artist who is best known for her dedication in pioneering feminist art. As an art instructor at Fresno State University in the early seventies Chicago developed an art education program for women.

In 1974–1979 Chicago turned her attention to the subject of women's history to create her most well-known work, *The Dinner Party,* which was executed between 1974 and 1979 with the participation of hundreds of volunteers. This monumental multimedia project was a symbolic representation of the history of women in Western Civilization and their contributions. Chicago painted ceramic plates; each plate depicted images of women and their important roles in history and arranged them on a table.

From 1980 to 1985, Chicago concentrated on childbirth and designed many images that were created for tapestry. Hundreds of women throughout the United States helped execute the needlework.

The Holocaust Project: From Darkness Into Light, which premiered in October 1993 at the Spertus Museum in Chicago, continues to travel to museums around the United States. The Holocaust Project, which grew out of eight years of inquiry, travel, study, and artistic creation, includes a series of images that merge Chicago's painting with the photography of Donald Woodman, as well as works in stained glass and tapestry designed by Chicago and executed by skilled artisans.

In 1996 the Arthur and Elizabeth Schlesinger Library on the History of Women in America at Radcliffe College, Cambridge, Massachusetts, chose to store all of Chicago's papers. This is a singular honor as Chicago is the first living artist to be included in this major archive.

In the fall of 1999, Chicago returned to teaching for the first time in 25 years, having accepted a succession of one-semester appointments at various institutions around the country, beginning with Indiana University where she received a presidential appointment in art and gender studies. In the fall of 2000, Chicago taught one course each at Duke University and the University of North Carolina.

For over three decades, Chicago has remained committed to the power of art as a vehicle for social change and to a woman's right to engage in the highest level of art production. As a result, her legacy will be that she brought the role of women in the arts to the forefront.

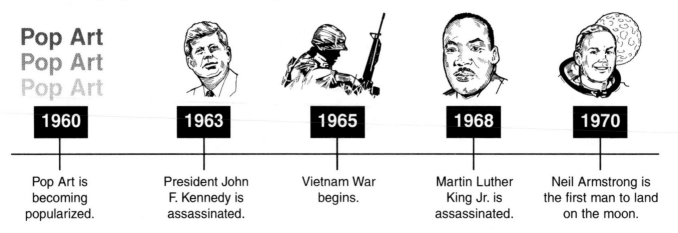

Pop Art
Pop Art
Pop Art

1960	1963	1965	1968	1970
Pop Art is becoming popularized.	President John F. Kennedy is assassinated.	Vietnam War begins.	Martin Luther King Jr. is assassinated.	Neil Armstrong is the first man to land on the moon.

The Dinner Party

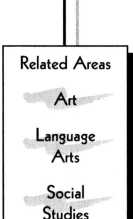
Focus

Students learn to create a dinner party to honor famous men, women, and children in American history.

Activity

learning to create in a circular motif using mixed medias

Vocabulary

ceramics, banner, biography, mixed media, contour, circular, motif, repetitive

Materials

2 white, black, or solid color tablecloths (fabric, sheets, etc.); white ceramic dinner plates (accumulate through garage sales, donations, secondhand stores)

Implementation

Day 1

1. Discuss and show transparency or prints of Judy Chicago and her exhibit of *The Dinner Party*.

2. Explain that students are going to create their own dinner party with famous men, women, or children of a certain period in history. (*Suggestion:* Use a period in history that is being currently studied)

3. Have them list people and put names on chart paper. (Have your own list in case of mind blanks.)

4. Each student selects a person to represent.

Day 2

1. Give students time to research their famous person and write a short paragraph highlighting the famous actions of the person.

2. Have students type the paragraph on the computer and then glue it onto a 6" x 13" place card and frame.

Day 3

1. Students are given a review lesson on drawing faces (see portrait painting and contour drawing). Practice drawing pictures of famous people using the contour method, keeping in mind the fashions in history. (i.e., Did they wear hats? What was the fashion and hair styles of the period?) Remember this contour portrait will be in a circular format and, for more interest, include neck and shoulders.

The Dinner Party

Implementation *(cont.)*

Days 4–5

1. Transfer the contour portrait in a circular format using a fine felt-tip, black marker onto the plate. The outer rim of the plate could have a circular, repeated pattern of objects of significance to the subject. (Think of it as a frame for subject.) Show samples of plates with repeat patterns. Paint on the plate with ceramic paints and markers.

2. Bake in oven using the directions that come with the ceramic markers. (Because this project involves using computers, paints, and oven, you may want to divide class into groups.)

Day 6

1. Arrange 4 long tables in a V-shape and cover with black or solid color tablecloths, fabric, or sheets. Have students set the tables with their plates. Put place cards above each plate. *Optional:* Set the mood with music of the time period and lighting.

Day 7

Invite other classes and parents to come see.

Extended Activities

1. If time or money is at a premium, you can substitute white paper plates (heavy duty) and crayons and markers for ceramic plates and paints.

2. Students create a dinner party honoring their mother or favorite female in their life for Mother's Day—drawing their portrait in the middle of the plate and using the subjects favorite flower as a repetitive motif around the outer rim of the plate.

3. Write a poem and put on a framed place card behind the plate. Invite mothers to tea and view the dinner party. At the end of viewing, students get to keep the poem and plate.

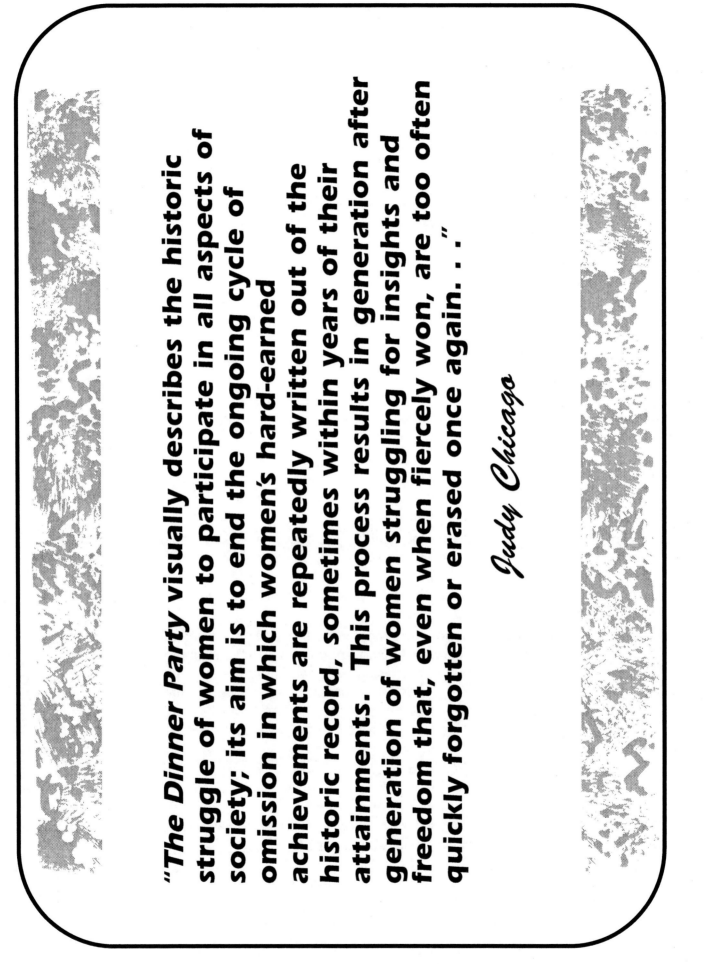

"The Dinner Party visually describes the historic struggle of women to participate in all aspects of society; its aim is to end the ongoing cycle of omission in which women's hard-earned achievements are repeatedly written out of the historic record, sometimes within years of their attainments. This process results in generation after generation of women struggling for insights and freedom that, even when fiercely won, are too often quickly forgotten or erased once again. . ."

Judy Chicago

1970s at a Glance

The seventies was a time of celebration as well as a time of political and social unrest. Our country was celebrating its 200th birthday in this decade while scandal was prominent in our nation's capital. President Richard Milhous Nixon became the first president to resign from office. Members of his cabinet were found bugging the democratic headquarters at the Watergate Hotel. Vice President Gerald Ford took over as president, but he was unable to win the election in 1976. James E. Carter, Jr. became the 39th president on January, 1977.

Exploration into space was continuing and on May 14, 1973, the United States launched *Skylab,* its first space station. Over the next nine months, three different crews lived inside the orbiting space craft. In 1978 astronomer James W. Christy discovered the moons of Pluto.

The women's movement was probably the greatest social change of the seventies decade. Gloria Steinem became the mentor for millions of women who wanted the same rights as men to succeed outside the home if they so chose. Bella Abzug became a crusader for equal rights for everyone, and Marian Wright Edelman was an active crusader for the rights of children.

Sports fans saw Babe Ruth's home run record broken by Hank Aaron. Muhammed Ali won the world title record in boxing three times, and Jack Nicklaus was becoming a golf legend in his own right. Robyn Smith became the first woman to ride a horse to victory at New York's Aqueduct Track.

Leroy Neiman was introducing the world to famous celebrities as seen through his eyes as a painter. He gained even greater recognition as the official artist of the Olympic Games. On close examination, his images seem to be abstract. Viewed from a distance, however, the shapes become dynamic figures that interact and move with great energy.

Jacob Lawrence became one of the most important African-American painters of his time. His pictures of migration of African Americans and the struggle of the working-class put him in a class of his own. He also drew pictures of such famous black heroes such as John Brown, Frederick Douglass, and Harriet Tubman. Jacob Lawrence spent his later years teaching at the University of Washington as well as painting. He was actively involved with his community and thrived on getting children involved with painting.

The seventies brought about many changes in America's attitudes and lifestyles. It became the era of the "Me, myself, and I" generation. It was a time of self-reflection, exercise, and eating foods for health and beauty. The environment was becoming an issue and many environment activist groups were trying to save the lands, birds, and environment through demonstrations and protests.

Faith Ringgold   Born 1930–

Art has always played an important role in Faith Ringgold's life. She was born in Harlem in 1930. Faith's mother introduced her to the world of art at an early age. Faith had developed asthma and spent much of her childhood in bed. Her mother made sure she had lots of books to read as well as paper and crayons for drawing. Faith often visited the art museums of New York with her mother as well as watching performing artists such as Duke Ellington and Billie Holiday at the Paramount Theater. Faith attended New York City College, majoring in art. Although Faith learned to copy the great artists of the past, she developed her own style by combining her European training with the symmetry, repetition, pattern, and texture of African art.

Faith refers to her art as an expression of the African-American female experience. Quilt making has been an important part of the African-American woman. Part of a female slave's job was to make quilts for the plantation owners. They then used the scraps left over for their own family. Faith chose this medium as a way to express her artistic talents. Art History, family, and friends are an integral part of the subject matter of her painted story quilts. In *Dancing at the Louvre,* the children in the picture are her own grandchildren.

Faith has always believed she could do anything. "No" has never been a word that has held her back. Although she is best known for her quilts, Faith has made soft sculptures and masks and is a children's book author. Her quilts portray people achieving their dreams and their goals. Putting her story quilts into books for children has brought the African American experience into the homes of millions of children. Her art has been displayed in museums all over the world, and her books have won numerous awards. Most importantly, her books and quilts, beside having told the history of the African-American to the world, exhibit the strength and courage of African-American woman.

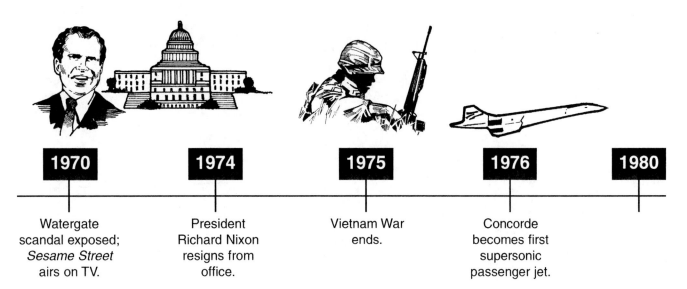

1970	**1974**	**1975**	**1976**	**1980**
Watergate scandal exposed; *Sesame Street* airs on TV.	President Richard Nixon resigns from office.	Vietnam War ends.	Concorde becomes first supersonic passenger jet.	

Textile Design

Related Areas

Art

Social
Studies

Geography

Focus

Students will be exposed to textile design in a variety of cultures.

Activity

Students will use meaningful symbols in repeat patterns of West Africa to make an Akan Adinkra cloth ("saying good-by cloth").

Vocabulary

diluted, symbols, poetic, banner, repetitive, quiltmaking, storytelling, textile, design

Materials

crayons; muslin; diluted brown tempera paint; variety of sizes of paintbrushes; symbols; posters with African textiles

Implementation

Day 1

Groups of students will read about Faith Ringgold and quilt making with an emphasis of groups and cultures participating in textile design. Allow about 15 minutes. Display posters of her quilts and those of other countries.

Have a discussion about community life in West African tribes. Display samples of the Akan Adinkar cloth. Explain the meaning behind the cloth. Emphasize the vocabulary.

Day 2

1. African designs are based on bold geometric shapes and repetitive lines. Use crayons to draw rows of Adinkar Symbols along with geometric shapes. Students may draw the symbols first with a pencil. A heavy application of crayon then needs to be applied.

2. After the muslin is covered with the crayon designs, stdunts dip the entire cloth into a solution of diluted tempera paint and then they squeeze the water from the cloth and lay it flat to dry.

Textile Design *(cont.)*

Extended Activity

Materials

Tar Beach by Faith Ringgold; white pillow cas; glue sticks; crayon overwriters; markers; glue; fabric paint; glitter

Make a Story Quilt Wall Hanging

1. Introduce the artist Faith Ringgold and her story *Tar Beach.* Discuss the closeness of family and/or friends.

2. Students focus on a work of art created out of paint and fabric rather than paint and paper, and they explore patterns by overlapping color and design.

3. Students make a border of a variety of patterns or pictures.

4. They first draw a design on paper showing the closeness of friends or family.

5. Teachers or parents stuff and stitch down open side.

6. Teachers or parents stitch on top and make loops for students to place on top of story quilt to hang.

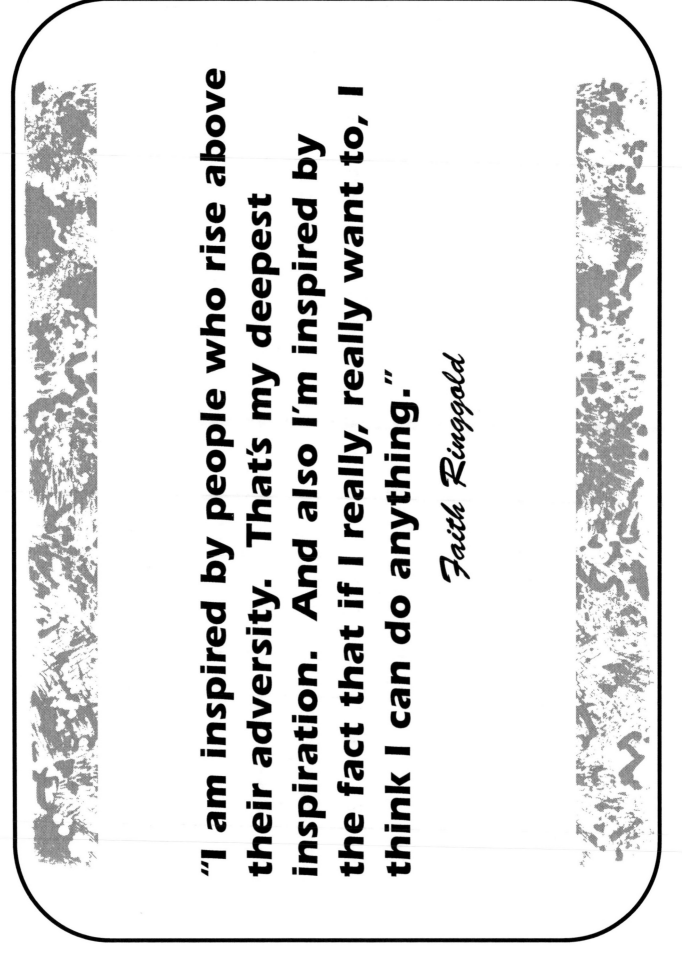

"I am inspired by people who rise above their adversity. That's my deepest inspiration. And also I'm inspired by the fact that if I really, really want to, I think I can do anything."

Faith Ringgold

74

Chuck Close   Born 1940–

Chuck Close is one of America's most celebrated artists, an achievement that might cause many who knew him as a child to shake their heads in total astonishment.

Born in Tacoma, Washington, in 1940, Close grew up in a time when a child who had trouble reading or staying on task was labeled difficult or slow. Chuck, himself, often felt overwhelmed by school, but never gave in to those feelings. He would spend hours in a darkened bathroom reading an assignment over and over until he could say it well enough to pass a test the next day. Today, his inability to read or see words as others do is known as *dyslexia,* a term not known in the '40s and '50s.

Drawing became an outlet for Close to be successful at an early age. Close has often said that it was his reading problem that helped him become such a successful artist.

Close's high school counselors discouraged him from attending college because of his low scores, but he decided to go ahead and apply to a two-year college in Tacoma, a decision that turned out to be a turning point in his education. The two-year institute had an excellent art department and the teachers were very encouraging to budding young artists. At first, Close thought he wanted to become an illustrator for Disney. After a few art classes, however, he knew that he wanted to become a painter. From the two-year college, he continued his education at the University of Washington and later the Yale University School of Art.

Close was enjoying a successful career as a realist painter when in 1988, he suffered a collapsed spinal artery that left him paralyzed from the shoulders down. Everyone thought that his career as a renowned artist had ended. After three years of learning to work past his physical condition, however, Chuck Close was back in the work world better than ever. His portraits took on a more impressionistic style and dynamic vision of the gridded black and white portrait. They were stronger and bolder. Where once they were in black and white, they now exploded into brightly patterned canvases.

Chuck Close continues to paint and people continue to be amazed at this artist who was labeled as "dumb," "lazy," and a "slow learner."

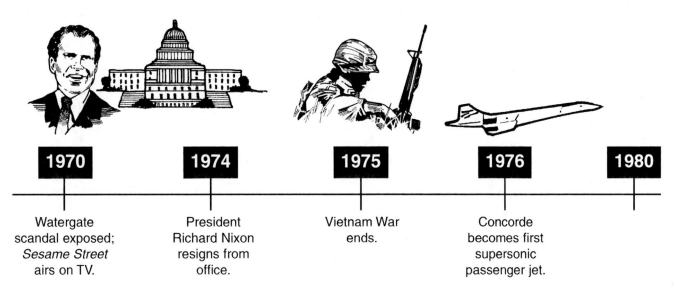

1970	1974	1975	1976	1980
Watergate scandal exposed; *Sesame Street* airs on TV.	President Richard Nixon resigns from office.	Vietnam War ends.	Concorde becomes first supersonic passenger jet.	

Grid Painting

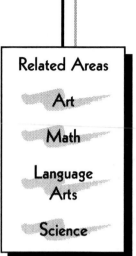

Related Areas

Art

Math

Language Arts

Science

Focus

Students become aware of the Photo Realism and Portraiture through the words of Chuck Close.

Activity

Using a grid students reproduce a photograph twice its size.

Vocabulary

portrait, composition, sketch, grid, pattern, design, positive space, negative space, primary colors, morph

Materials

a video about Chuck Close; posters of Chuck Close and his paintings; poster examples of Close's work; photos of faces from magazines; mirrors; rulers; 8" x 10" and 16" x 20" drawing paper ; pencils; crayons; markers; paints and brushes; 8" x 10" inch grid photocopied on film; graphite pencils of various sizes; tracing paper

Implementation

Day 1

1. Discuss life of Chuck Close emphasizing his overcoming physical challenges and show video of Chuck Close and prints of Chuck Close's paintings.

2. Each student selects a large photograph or magazine print of a person that is provided to make a grid portrait.

Days 2–5

1. Distribute a ruler, paper, and grid to each student. Using a ruler, the student makes a 2-inch grid lightly drawn on 16"x 20" paper.

2. Student lays the grid on the photo of the person.

3. Drawing with a pencil, each student transfers the image one square at a time from an 1-inch grid on an 8" x 10" to a 2-inch grid on a 16" x 20" paper, maintaining the same proportions.

4. After each student completes the transfer, he or she darkens using only graphite pencils.

5. Then the student mounts each drawing on black paper and then frames it with a white frame.

Grid Painting *(cont.)*

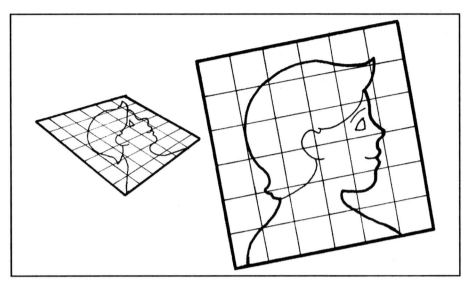

Extended Activities

Paint Grid Drawing

Students trace over grid and carbon transfer onto water color paper and paint using only the primary colors.

Self-Portrait

Using a mirror each student draws a self portrait in pencil using the contour method and then fill in with details in pencil.

Grid Name

1. Students create a grid using pencils and rulers on any sheet of paper that will fit their names (for first time use 3-inch grids).

2. Then they bubble letter their names on the grid, lightly in pencil.

3. Within each square space needs to be considered inside or outside the letter of the space within the grid. Using a complementary color scheme (1 primary and its complement), color inside spaces 1 color and outside spaces another color, then the name can be seen as the color selection reveals it!

Extensions

The grid activity can be used to reinforce color concepts, such as analogous colors, complementary colors, etc. It is also a natural extension of math concepts of measurement and using a ruler.

Extended Technology Activity

Scan a self-portrait image into a graphics program such as *Adobe Photoshop* and morph, using *Artistic Effects*.

"Art saved my life."

"Everyday when I roll out of the studio and look over my shoulder I say, 'That's what I did today.'"

Chuck Close

1980s at a Glance

The eighties saw many changes. The United States was enjoying a strong economy. The technological advances were beginning to revolutionize American business as well as the American family. Families were being introduced to VCRs, CD players, and personal computers. Telephones were available that could take messages and cable television broadened the spectrum of television viewing options. Families were beginning to experience a breakdown in the ability to live with simple comforts and were looking towards technology to make their lives easier.

Science was making enormous advances in the area of health and longevity. New advances in medicine was making it possible to replace hearts, kidneys, and other vital organs. Space travel was becoming more and more common as well as more expensive. The Space Transportation System was developed to create reusable spacecraft to reduce the cost. On April 12, 1981, the first operational shuttle, *Columbia*, went into orbit. The shuttle circled the earth 36 times over a period of two days. Scientific equipment was used to run a series of tests. The sixth shuttle flight was performed by the *Challenger* in 1983. The *Challenger* completed a total of nine flights, but during its tenth flight in January of 1986, it exploded in less than 80 seconds after takeoff. The seven members of the space shuttle were all killed, one of whom was a civilian named Christa McAuliffe, a high school teacher. The space shuttle program was halted until the problem could be corrected. Finally, in 1988, the program resumed with the shuttle *Discovery*.

The sports of the eighties were centered around the Olympic Games. In 1980 the Winter Olympics were held in Lake Placid, New York. The U.S. hockey team took home the first gold medal ever won in hockey for the United States.

The Summer Olympics of the same year were boycotted by our country and several others for the invasion of Afghanistan by Russia. The Summer Olympics of 1988 in Seoul, South Korea, however, were attended by the United States. Track stars Florence Griffith-Joyner and Jackie Joyner-Kersee were two prominent athletes who represented the United States during the Olympic Games.

The music world saw the rise of many artists who had their own brand of music. Michael Jackson, once a member of the Jackson Five, became a super star in his own right. Madonna also used her distinctive style as a singer and dancer to create videos that spotlighted her talent. Both stars used their ability to be totally outrageous and unpredictable to produce one-of-a-kind videos.

The artist and architect Maya Lin became a celebrity by submitting her idea for a new memorial honoring veterans of the Vietnam War. Maya Lin's entry was chosen and became one of the famous landmarks in Washington, D.C.

Maya Lin   ## Born 1959–

Maya Lin, a renowned architect and artist, created the Vietnam Veteran's Memorial, recognized by the millions who go to Washington, D.C. each year to visit her famous work.

Born October, 10, 1959, in Athens, Ohio, she earned a master's degree in architecture from Yale in 1986. At the young age of 21, Maya Lin won the open competition to create a memorial to the American Vietnam Veterans in Washington, D.C.

Her creation was different from the traditional memorial. Therefore, she met with a lot of controversy and skepticism in the beginning from veterans groups as well as politicians. Many wanted her to change or alter her basic design for they did not understand that her design conveyed the message they actually wanted. Some even called her design, "dishonorable" and "a scar." Maya Lin, however, could not be persuaded to change her design. She had a vision and this vision was not to be altered or changed by those who could not see what her creative eye could.

In 1981 her creation was unveiled. The memorial was two, large V-shaped, black granite walls reflected in a pool, appearing from a distance to be sunken in the earth, with the names of 57,661 Americans who died in the Vietnam War.

Maya Lin has created other notable memorials. To her credit she was chosen to design a memorial that chronicles the history of the Civil Rights Movement and 40 people killed between May 17, 1954 (when the Supreme Court outlawed school segregation), and April 4, 1968 (the assassination of Dr. Martin Luther King, Jr.), for the Civil Rights Movement. Lin worked on a design that would encourage reflection as well as educate those who saw it. A circular, black granite table records the names of 40 martyrs and chronicles the history of the Civil Rights Movement in lines that radiate like the hands of a clock. Water also cascades over a curved, black granite wall behind the table. Engraved on the wall are works paraphrased from the *Book of Amos* that Dr. King quoted on several occasions: "…until justice rolls down like waters and righteousness like a mighty stream."

Today, Maya Lin owns a successful design studio in New York.

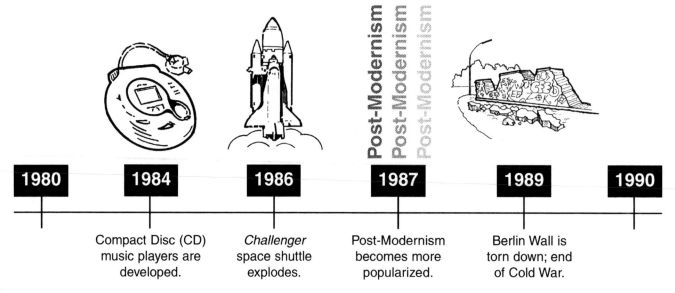

1980	1984	1986	1987	1989	1990
	Compact Disc (CD) music players are developed.	*Challenger* space shuttle explodes.	Post-Modernism becomes more popularized.	Berlin Wall is torn down; end of Cold War.	

Family History

Related Areas

Art

Language
Arts

Social
Studies

Focus

Developing an appreciation of family history.

Activity

Students create a mural/timeline about their family history

Vocabulary

timeline, statue, monument, historical, 3-dimensional, diorama

Materials

36' x 90' white butcher paper; pencil; chalk; paint; crayons; colored pencils; newspaper clippings; copies of family photos

Implementation

Day 1

1. Brainstorm with the class the importance of their family and how every family is important to the growth and development of a country.

2. Read a short biography of Maya Lin. Discuss the importance of the Vietnam War Memorial. Emphasize the struggle that the young Asian woman went through after winning a national contest with her design.

3. *Optional:* Ask a Vietnam vet to speak to your class.

4. Students write a biography of their family typewritten on the computer. Students mount copies of photos of their family members under the biography.

5. Show film clips about the Vietnam War and a biography of Maya Lin.

6. Divide a large piece of butcher paper in half. Have students type lists of their immediate family into the computer and glue each list on the butcher paper.

Family History *(cont.)*

Extended Activities

Materials

shoeboxes, construction paper, clay, pencil, paper

Design an outdoor monument for a famous person. (*Examples*: Lincoln Memorial, Statue of Liberty, Martin Luther King, Jr. Memorial, Washington Monument)

1. Show pictures of famous memorials.

2. Discuss famous people students think contributed to the U.S. in some way.

3. Students make a list of at least 5 people in history who have made a difference.

4. Students select a person, find photos and design a monument out of self-hardening clay to represent that person.

5. A written biography of a person, drawing of the design, and description of why this design was chosen to represent the person is to go along with the monument.

6. Students construct a diorama from a shoebox to set the stage for their monuments. They draw or collect photos of the surrounding area and place them in the shoebox. The 3-D design is to be placed in or in front of a diorama. Display in a prominent area.

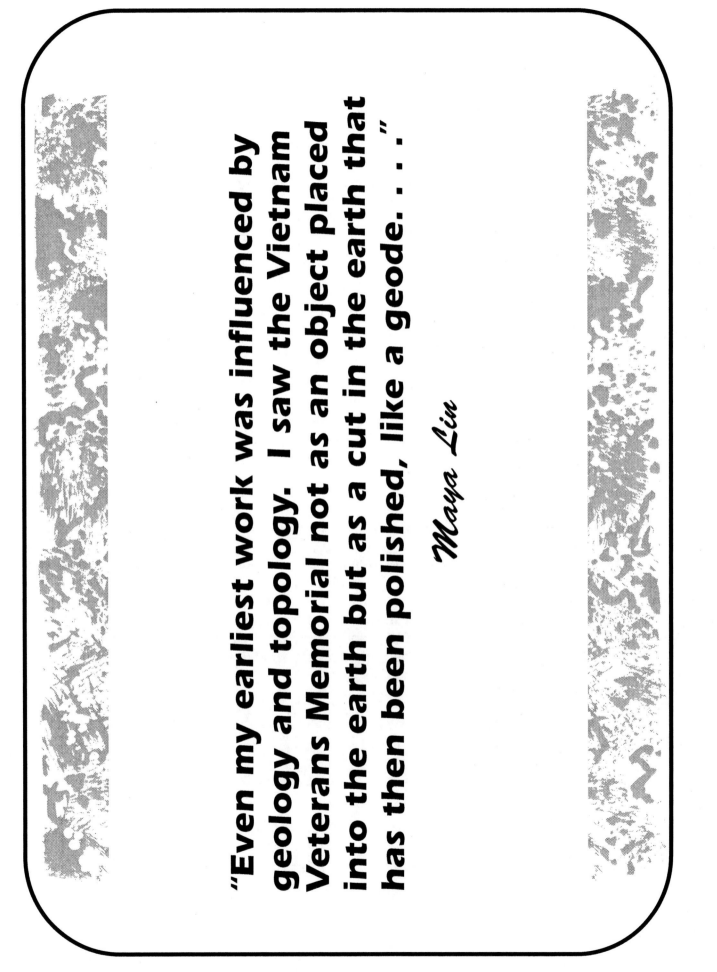

"Even my earliest work was influenced by geology and topology. I saw the Vietnam Veterans Memorial not as an object placed into the earth but as a cut in the earth that has then been polished, like a geode. . . ."

Maya Lin

Judith Baca   Born 1946–

Judith Baca was born in 1946 into a household where the women played a dominant role in her family. Baca showed an early interest in art, especially in the area of murals, but soon realized that the art of making murals did not have a prominent place in American art. She decided that she wanted to play an instrumental role in bringing murals into the American art scene. At the age of 31, Baca attended Taller Siqueiros in Curenavaca, Mexico, where she studied the technical aspects of working on murals.

One of Baca's most well known murals is *The Great Wall.* The project took seven years to complete. The 40 panels, which stretch across half a mile of the Tujunga Wash Flood Control Channel, was painted by the inner-city youth of this area. The mural depicts the history of the people of Los Angeles, and in particular, the Mexican-American community. It tells the story, decade by decade, of the contributions and struggles of California's diverse peoples from the beginning of the 1950s.

Baca has dedicated her life to making sure that public art works will become a part of every community. She started a program called SPARC (Special Arts Resource Centers) in 1981, of which she is still the director. The purpose of this program is to insure that America's diverse populations, including ethnic groups, women in careers, youth, and elderly are not forgotten or ignored. Her diligent and never wavering efforts have produced over 250 murals throughout the Los Angeles area.

Baca has traveled with her one-woman show across the country, lecturing and talking about the importance of recording a community's history through art. She is often asked to be the keynote speaker for different organizations as well as serve on many museum boards.

True to her mission, Baca is presently working on a commission for the Denver International Airport titled *World Wall: A Vision of the Future Without Fear.* This mural will be 210-feet long when completed and will address contemporary issues of global importance: war, peace, cooperation, and spiritual growth. It will include seven parts and will be shown around the world. Seven different artists will add additional panels to the work in a visual tribute to the "Global Village," proof that one person can make a difference to the world around them.

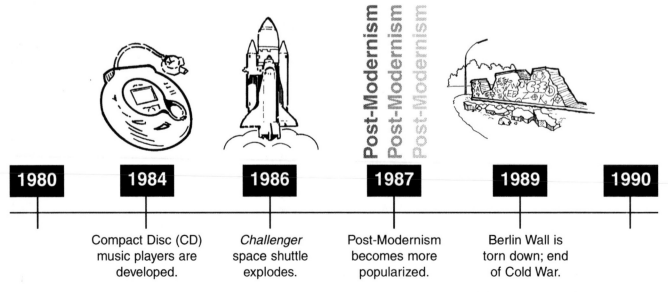

1980	1984	1986	1987	1989	1990
	Compact Disc (CD) music players are developed.	*Challenger* space shuttle explodes.	Post-Modernism becomes more popularized.	Berlin Wall is torn down; end of Cold War.	

Murals

Related Areas

Art

Language Arts

Physical Education

Science

Social Studies

Focus

Students learn that murals are images on walls, building exteriors and interiors, and other large public surfaces.

Activity

Students will create their own mural dealing with an important historical event.

Vocabulary

mural, images, persuasion, responsibility

Materials

large pieces of butcher paper; crayons; tempera paint; brushes; chalk; pencils

Implementation

Day 1

1. Facilitate a discussion about Judith Baca with the class, using a biography as a reading assignment. It is important to emphasize that murals are large images on walls that are usually used to influence the viewer to think about a political issue in a certain way.

2. Review the historical event(s) that the class has been studying. Inform students that they will be divided into cooperative learning groups and will plan, draw, and color a mural.

3. Write on chart paper or transparency the necessary criteria to be considered in producing the mural. Have students sign up for the event they wish to draw (i.e., Boston Tea Party, Bunker Hill, Signing of the Declaration of Independence, etc.).

Day 2

1. Go over the rules of making a mural with the whole class. Post or put up a transparency of the following mural directions:

    a. Decide as a group whether you want your mural to show a positive or negative side to the historical event.

    b. Discuss the event as to people, things, and landscapes. Decide which part each member of the group will take.

    c. Tape a large sheet of butcher paper to the chalkboard and plan how you are going to go about sketching your picture (i.e., how many can work on it at a time, what are everyone's tasks?).

    d. Sketch the people and events onto the butcher paper lightly so that any mistakes can be erased. When the mural has been completely sketched, it is ready to be colored.

Murals *(cont.)*

Implementation *(cont.)*

Day 2 *(cont.)*

    e. Use crayons, paint, or chalk. The materials you wish to use are at the art center. More than one type of medium can be used. Use your imagination and be creative!

    f. When the mural is complete, hang it in the designated class area or school area.

Extended Activities

1. Explain that murals are images on walls or building exteriors and interiors and that mural makers use various techniques. Use a picture of a Diego Rivera fresco and a Judith Baca mural to illustrate two different mural painting processes.

2. Students examine Chicano murals and earlier murals made for protest and persuasion. After an introduction to two mural-making processes, students consider the responsibilities that different people can take in that process.

Objectives

1. Students learn that murals are images on walls or building exteriors and interiors and other large, usually public, surfaces.

2. Students learn that mural makers use different techniques and media. (Some paint directly on surfaces, others paint on a plaster coating applied to the existing surface. This last technique is called fresco painting.)

3. Students learn how to identify individual tasks that must be coordinated in order to complete a large mural.

4. Students learn that artists sometimes choose mural making as a method for communicating to large numbers of people.

5. Students learn that Chicano and earlier artists from Mexico have a strong mural-making tradition.

6. Students can make small (9" x 14") drawings on their own using the style of either Judith Baca or Diego Rivera. Make a bulletin board displaying the two different styles.

7. Using the murals of Diego Rivera as examples, have students produce a chalk mural using the style of Rivera.

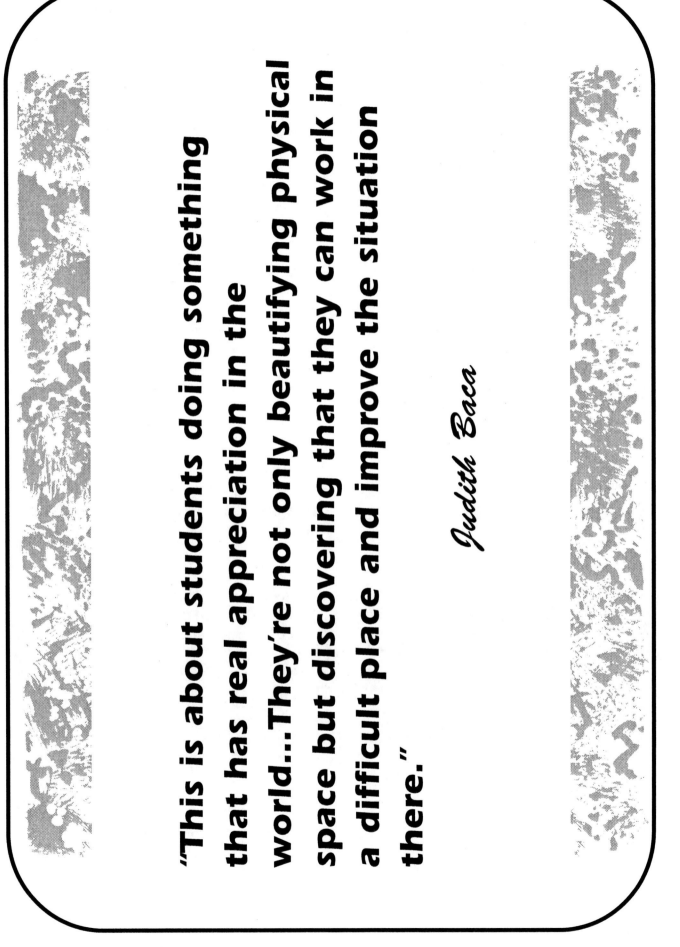

"This is about students doing something that has real appreciation in the world...They're not only beautifying physical space but discovering that they can work in a difficult place and improve the situation there."

Judith Baca

1990s at a Glance

The decade opened with the fall of the Union of the Soviet Socialist Republics (U. S. S. R.), followed by restructuring and civil wars throughout the former Soviet Republic. In Russia, Mikhail Gorbachev, the Soviet leader who had been instrumental in bringing about the change, fell out of power and a new era, under the leadership of Boris Yeltsin and others, began. War tore apart the nation of Bosnia-Hercegovina, once a part of Yugoslavia, in the aftermath of the Soviet Republic's demise. Meanwhile, in South Africa, former political prisoner Nelson Mandela became president and apartheid (i.e., racial inequality and separation) ended.

This decade saw the Persian Gulf War (Operation Desert Storm) waged in early 1991 between Iraq and a coalition of 39 nations organized by the United States and the United Nations. The beginning of the war was the invasion of Kuwait by Iraq. This invasion led to fears that Iraq would attempt to invade a neighboring country, Saudi Arabia. Because much of the global oil production was tied to this region of the Middle East, the United Nations Security Council agreed to use "all necessary means" to dispel Iraq from Kuwait. The war ended in April 11, 1991 with Iraq withdrawing its military from Kuwait.

Other points of interest include the birth of the World Wide Web and increased global Internet use. Janet Reno became the first female U.S. Attorney General while Madeline Albright became the first female Secretary of State. Michael Jordan and the Chicago Bulls won six NBA championships during the 1990s and Mark McGwire broke baseball's single-season, homerun record in 1998. In golf Tiger Woods rose to prominence during the latter half of the 1990s.

This decade also saw Hong Kong returned to China from British sovereignty and Panama gain control of the Panama Canal from the U.S. On the scientific front, the Hubble Space Telescope was released for space exploration and the Mars *Pathfinder* landed on Mars to gather information about the red planet. This was also the era that saw the passing of international figures such as Mother Teresa, King Hussein of Jordan, Frank Sinatra, and England's Princess Diana.

The 1990s was an era of economic prosperity and technological innovation. It witnessed the rise of the Internet or "dot com" businesses and saw people connecting with people in different parts of the world via e-mail, video conferencing, etc. Yet this era may only be the cusp of the technological revolution.

Luis Jimenez

Born 1940–

Luis Jimenez was born in El Paso, Texas. His family came from Mexico to the United States in search of a better life. Jimenez grew up in the barrio of El Paso, Texas, and learned to appreciate the arts at an early age watching, as well as helping his father who was a sign painter and neon maker. His family was poor, but his love of art continued to thrive through reading about art and visiting the wonderful art galleries in Mexico City.

The art galleries of Mexico City gave him a love and appreciation for his culture. He developed a great sense of appreciation for the Hispanic artists of the past and present.

He attended the University of Texas and graduated in 1964. He started out in the field of architecture but eventually turned to the area of drawing and sculpture. Through his studies, he became fascinated with the forms and expressive qualities of the Baroque style of sculpture. He began his career by focusing on fiberglass sculptures of American cars, music, and dance with an emphasis on the Hispanic contribution. His sculptures were bold, colorful and often reached heights of seven to ten feet or more. He spent a great deal of time refining their surfaces until they were smooth and luminous as in the Baroque style.

Towards the end of the 1960s, he turned his attention toward the southwest. He completed several sculptures of the American Indian, cowboy, and Mexican migrant worker. His images of the cowboy, Indian and immigrant are often involved in action, such as bucking broncos, on the dance floor, or struggling across the border. His sculpture of the Vaquero reminds us that the first American cowboys were Mexican in origin. His sculptures *Border Crossing* and *Southwest Pieta* help the viewer understand the sacrifice many Mexicans have endured trying to gain their freedom.

Besides his sculptures of people, Jimenez has tried to show the southwest as a place of great beauty where people and animals live together in harmony rather than at odds with one another. His choices of color subject intertwine to bring the idea of harmony and balance.

Jimenez has also worked in watercolors, pencil drawings, and prints. He completed a series of portraits on his family members, friends, as well as himself. Here, his subjects show the more introspective side of the artist. Jimenez continues today to work as an artist in his home in Hondo, New Mexico, where he resides with his wife and their three children. His works continue to inspire and educate those who view them in art galleries throughout the U.S.

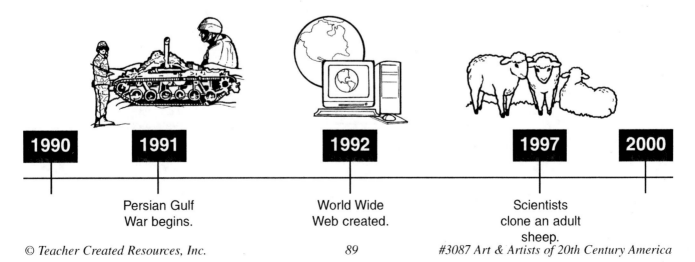

1990	1991	1992	1997	2000
	Persian Gulf War begins.	World Wide Web created.	Scientists clone an adult sheep.	

Cowboys and Cowgirls

Related Areas

Art

Language Arts

Social Studies

Focus

Develop an understanding of the real American cowboy and cowgirl as opposed to the romantic portrayal.

Activity

Group activities include researching history, biographies, articles of clothing, day-to-day life, and artifacts of cowboys and cowgirls of all ethnic backgrounds in the "Wild Wild West." These activities are to culminate in display boards for a "Western Museum" to be viewed by peers.

Vocabulary

complementary colors, monochromatic colors, branding, logo design, artifacts, exhibit display

Materials

pencil; display boards; large sheets of butcher paper; glue; spray mount; colored paper; video of *High Noon*; video of a cowboy cartoon

Implementation

Day 1

1. Introduce students to cowboys and cowgirls and discuss and list famous cowboys/cowgirls in real life, comic books, TV, and film.

2. Introduce students to western history in a library and/or using the Internet.

3. Show examples of exhibit displays.

4. Go to a western museum (e.g., Autry Museum in Los Angeles, California).

5. Divide students into groups. Then each group selects a leader and divides out responsibilities for each requirement in the display: brand for ranch, draw character and indicate name of all articles of clothing, photos, artifacts of day-to-day life, and written biography of assigned cowboy or cowgirl.

Cowboys and Cowgirls *(cont.)*

Implementation *(cont.)*

Day 2

1. Discuss logo design (everyday brands such as Coke®, IBM®, Apple®, etc.).

2. Show examples of ranch brands.

3. Students draw a brand of their display.

Day 3

1. Draw an outline around a student who lies down on butcher paper. Use this as a model for cowboy or cowgirl by drawing western articles of clothing (to be clearly labeled).

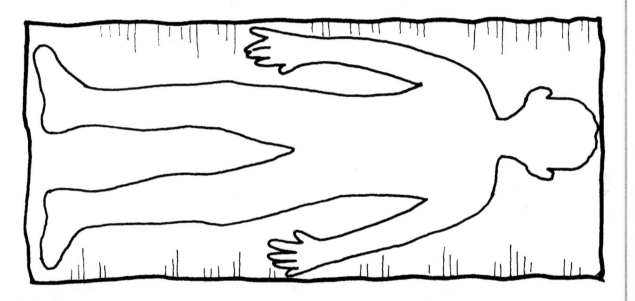

Days 4–6

Mount and display western invitations for school.

Extended Activities

1. Act out and film a western.

2. Make a cartoon strip of a cowboy.

3. Make food of the west (e.g., no-bake Cowpie Cookies).

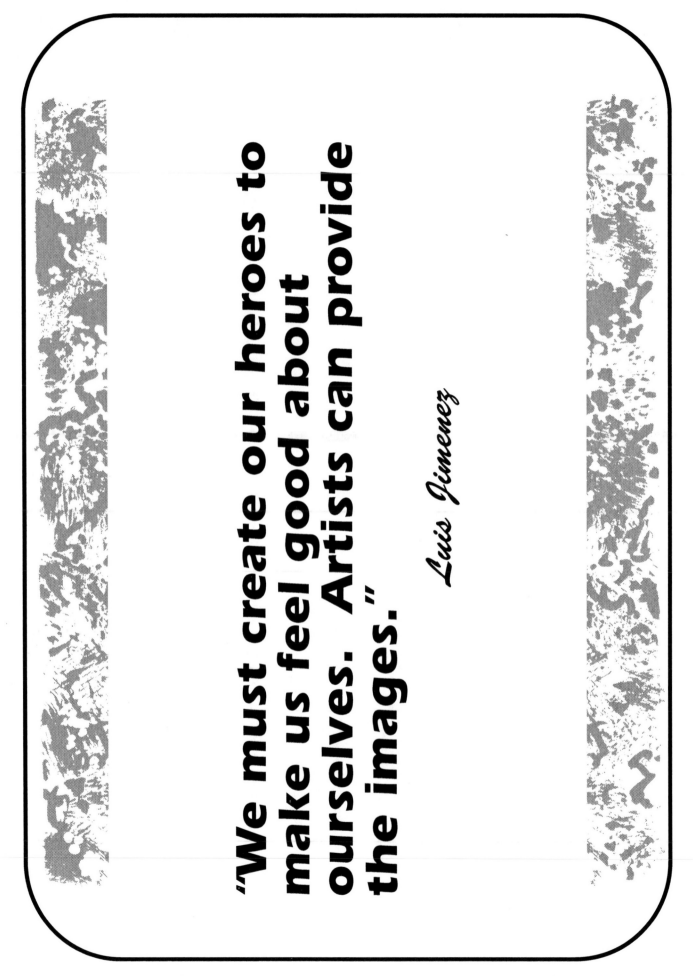

"We must create our heroes to make us feel good about ourselves. Artists can provide the images."

Luis Jimenez

George Lucas

Born 1944–

George Lucas was born on May 14, 1944, in Modesto, California. From the very beginning Lucas always loved creating his own world. He would often get his friends and family members to help him put on backyard carnivals. He was an avid fan of mythological characters and their adventures.

Lucas was obsessed with comic books, television, and racing cars. As a young teenager, he dreamed of becoming a race car driver after he graduated from high school. This dream ended, however, when his car flipped over and landed him in the hospital. Lucas graduated from high school while in the hospital and his dreams of becoming a race car driver ended. Instead, he decided to go to college.

Lucas's first two years of college were a struggle, until he started taking classes having to do with filmmaking. After two years at the local college, he entered UCLA, where he began taking more and more classes having to do with the motion picture industry. His grades and interest in college greatly improved, and he found himself spending more and more time producing and directing his own little films for his film classes. Soon films became his whole life. Upon graduation, Lucas received two scholarships, one of which was to observe film maker, Francis F. Coppola.

Coppola and Lucas became fast friends and decided to form their own company, which allowed them to produce their own films the way they wanted. They made several movies together, one being *American Graffiti* which was based somewhat on Lucas's own life. This movie gave Lucas his first big break. He went on to make two more big hits, *E.T.: The Extra Terrestrial* and *Star Wars*.

Next, Lucas decided to challenge himself with a science fiction movie, a subject that had always intrigued him. The title of this film was *Star Wars*. It was to have all the characteristics and elements of a myth or fairy tale, good triumphing over evil, mystical characters, and a fairy-tale-like ending. Making *Star Wars* was one of the most difficult challenges of his career because of all the special effects, music, actors, and locations of some of the scenes.

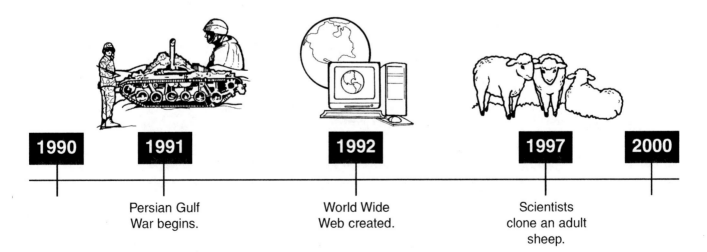

1990	1991	1992	1997	2000
	Persian Gulf War begins.	World Wide Web created.	Scientists clone an adult sheep.	

George Lucas

Born 1944–

Lucas was often discouraged, but he continued until the movie was completed. He hoped at least to get back the money he had put into the picture. Not only was *Star Wars* a huge success, but it was one of the highest grossing movies of that time. Lucas has gone on to fill the screen with two more *Star Wars* sequels, as well as a prequel. This time, however, he hired other talented artists to do some of the jobs that he had done.

Lucas has always taken his job and the effect of his movies on his audience seriously. For this reason, he has formed three companies, each with a different purpose in mind. Lucas Arts Entertainment Corporation provides schools and homes with computer programs for interactive learning. Lucas Digital Ltd. provides studios with visual effects and sound design in an atmosphere where film creators can be as creative as they want. His third company Lucas Film Ltd., has developed a THX sound system to improve the movie experience for the audience.

Lucas is a strong believer that creativity requires a work environment where creative people can explore their every fantasy. His devotion and concern for children and the effects of his movies on them is always an integral part of his work. He has created "The George Lucas Educational Foundation" because of his belief that education is vital to society.

Not only has he helped revolutionize and advance movie and film technology, George Lucas is truly an artist whose contributions live through his fairy tales and legendary movies.

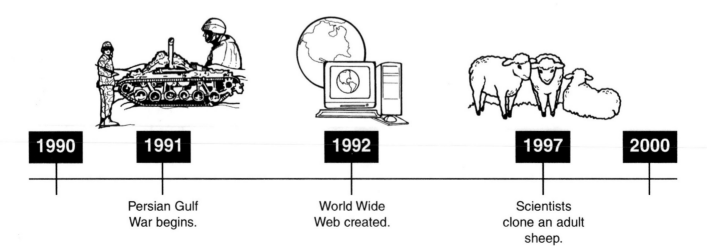

| 1990 | 1991 | 1992 | 1997 | 2000 |

Persian Gulf
War begins.

World Wide
Web created.

Scientists
clone an adult
sheep.

Filmmaking

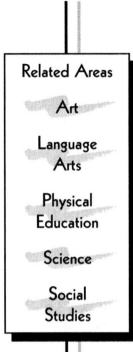

Related Areas

Art

Language Arts

Physical Education

Science

Social Studies

Focus

Students learn the process of making a documentary film.

Activity

produce a film demonstrating how to make or do something (play soccer, make a cake, etc.)

Vocabulary

crew, director, producer, script, documentary, icon, science fiction, special effects, storyboard, actors, credits, title

Materials

12" x 18" white paper; pencils; eraser; video camera; props selected by students; TV; VCR; film

Implementation

1. Introduce the filmmaking process to the class.

2. Have printed steps posted and hand out work sheets with film terminology and the filmmaking history of George Lucas.

3. Present a video that has been previewed and edited for this lesson.

4. Students watch the movie in class, paying close attention to the effects of sound, color, timing, editing, actors and credits.

5. Students are divided into groups of 3–5 (called a film crew).

6. Each film crew writes a story documenting how to do something and then makes the story into a storyboard.

7. Review each storyboard with its film crew before producing video/film.

8. Students select a setting, producer, cameraman, props, and backdrop. Actors within their group do the project several times so that each student has the opportunity to be in each role.

Extended Activities

1. Write and produce a video of a fairy tale or myth (science fiction).

2. Write and produce a video of a commercial for an everyday real or fictional product.

3. Write and produce a video news broadcast which includes a news anchor, sports broadcaster, and weather person.

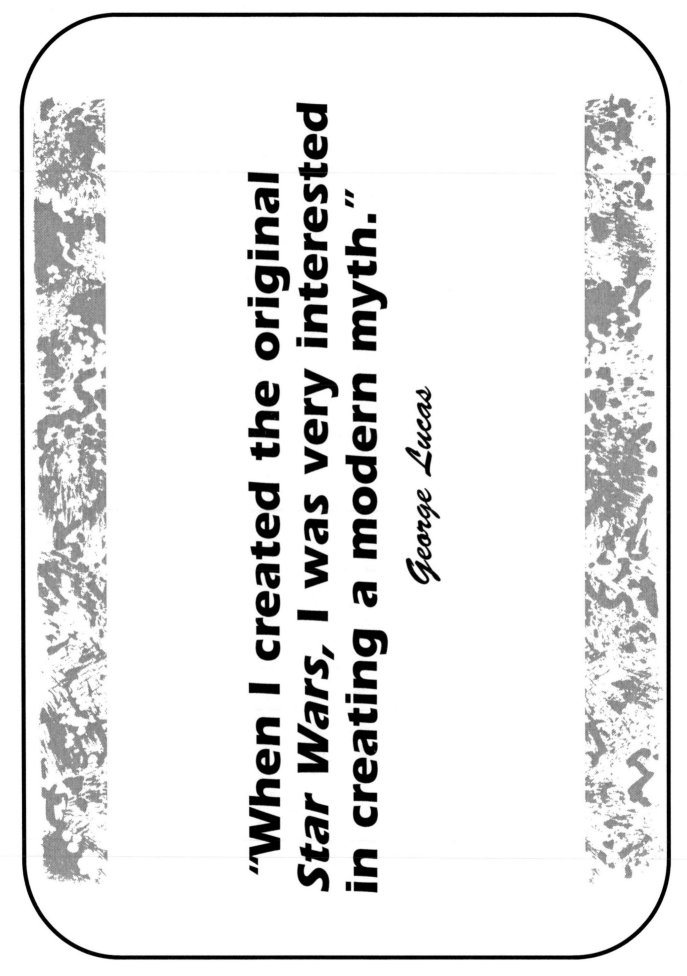

"When I created the original *Star Wars*, I was very interested in creating a modern myth."

George Lucas

Art Terms

animation–showing movement

balance–objects and space in a picture are equal

camera–an instrument used to take photographs or motion pictures

cartoon–a drawing that caricatures, often satirically, some situation or person; a comic strip

cell–one of thousands of small units of drawings that make up a cartoon feature film

character–what a person or thing is really like as shown by the way he or she thinks, talks, or acts

cinematographer–the person in charge of running the camera and filming the movie

color–red, orange, yellow, green, blue, indigo, violet

complementary–add to the essence of something else

composition–the arrangement of form, color, line, space, and mass in a work of art

crew–all of the people involved in the making of a movie

design–a plan or drawing that shows how something will look or will be made

documentary–a nonfiction film or photograph meant to be educational

editor–a person in charge of every aspect of a film

expressionism–a style of art which exaggerates or distorts shape, line, and color to portray the artistic feeling

figure–a shape that represents the human form

fine art–collective term to describe painting, drawing, and printmaking and sometimes also music and poetry

folk art–artwork which is done by an artist with no formal training

form (or **shape**)–the outline or external contour of an object

found object–a naturally-occurring or man-made object, such as driftwood, fabric, or a bottle which, unaltered, is either exhibited as an artistic object in its own right, or incorporated into a work of art

grip—the person in charge of props and carrying film equipment

hue—a color's name or its position in the spectrum

icon—a corporate identity or character that people admire

Art Terms *(cont.)*

impressionism—style of painting begun by a group of French artists at the end of the 19th century. The bright colors are applied freely to capture the effects of light.

intensity—brightness or dullness of a hue

line—a continuous mark or stroke (long, short, thick, straight, zigzagged, curved, looped, dotted)

mobile—a linear-hanging sculpture that moves. It was invented by Alexander Calder.

monument—statue or object that is built to honor some famous event or person

motion—movement of an object from one place to another

mural—a painting created for walls or ceilings

negative space—empty space in an artwork; a void

Op Art—a type of painting or drawing that concentrates on creating optical effects to convince our eyes that there is motion where there is none

perspective—a method of creating a sense of space and distance in a picture

photography—a means by which chemically sensitized surfaces are exposed to light and retain an image of what is in front of them

photomontage—a collage using photographs

Pop Art—art style centering on everyday objects that are incorporated into the artworks

positive space—space in an artwork that is filled with something, such as lines, designs, color, or shapes

post-production—the addition of sound, music, and special effects after a movie has been filmed

profile—view or outline of a certain figure

projection—to show an image on a screen

renaissance—period of history of the rebirth of art, literature, and learning in Europe during the 14th–17th centuries

science fiction—a story involving setting, characters, or technology that does not exist

score—music created for a movie

sculpture—three-dimensional art work

Art Terms *(cont.)*

shade—a color to which black or another dark hue has been added to make it darker. For example, black added to green makes it a darker shade of green. Value changes from pure hues are called *shades* and *tints*.

shape—an element of art, it is an enclosed space defined and determined by other art elements such as line, color, value, and texture. In painting and drawing, shapes may take on the appearance of solids (two dimensions)—length and width. This two-dimensional character of shape distinguishes it from form, which has depth as well as length and width.

sketch—a quick drawing that loosely captures the appearance or action of a place or situation. Sketches are often done in preparation for larger, more detailed works of art.

special effects—ways of making unreal or impossible situations believable

stabile—an abstract sculpture that has moveable parts similar to a mobile, but is attached to a solid, unmovable base rather than suspended

still life—in the visual arts, subject matter that is not living

Surrealism—an art movement which stressed the importance of the irrational and the subconscious. Surrealistic paintings usually look very strange and often disturbing.

symbol—a form, image or subject representing a meaning other than the one with which it is usually associated

symmetry—something that is balanced or even

textile—fabric or cloth made by weaving or knitting fibers

texture—the surface feeling or look of an object

three-dimensional—any object having height, width, and depth

timeline—list of events or people in chronological order

transparency—able to be seen through clearly

trilogy—a series of three films or three books

watercolor—a paint that is made by mixing color with water instead of oil

Art Resources

Here are some suggested books and/or videos that may be useful for classroom research.

Eadweard Muybridge

Muybridge, Eadweard, et al. *The Human Figure in Motion.* Dover Publications, 1989.

Muybridge, Eadweard. *Horses and Other Animals in Motion.* Dover Publications, 1985.

Muybridge, Eadweard. *The Male and Female Figure in Motion: 60 Classic Sequences.* Dover Publications, 1984.

Hart, Christopher. *How to Draw Cartoons for Comic Strips.* Watson-Guptill Publications, 1988.

Frederic Remington

Ballew, Emily Neff, Remington, Frederic, and Wynne Phelan. *Frederic Remington.* Princeton University Press, 2000.

Dippie, Brian W., Remington, Frederic and Frederic Remington Art Museum. *The Frederic Remington Art Museum Collection.* Harry N. Abrams, 2001.

Remington, Frederic. *The American West of Frederic Remington.* Andrew McMeel Publishing, 1994.

Frederic Remington: The Truth of Other Days. 58 minutes. 1990

Alfred Stieglitz

Bry, Doris. *Alfred Stieglitz: Photographer.* Museum of Fine Arts Boston/Bullfinch, 1996.

Greenough, Sara, et al. *Alfred Stieglitz: Photographs and Writings.* Bullfinch, 1999.

Naef, Weston J. *The Collection of Alfred Stieglitz: Fifty Pioneers of Modern Photography.* Metropolitan Museum/Viking, 1978.

Norman, Dorothy and Stieglitz, Alfred. *Alfred Stieglitz (Masters of Photography Series).* Aperture, 1997.

Frank Lloyd Wright

Jacobs, Herbert and Jacobs, Katherine. *Building with Frank Lloyd Wright.* Southern Illinois University Press, 1986.

Larkin, David (Ed.) and Pfeffier, Bruce Brooks. *Frank Lloyd Wright: The Masterworks.* Rizzoli, 1993.

Thomson, Iain, Wright, Frank Lloyd, and Maria Constantino. *Frank Lloyd Wright.* Thunder Bay Press, 1998.

Thomsen, Kathleen Thorne. *Frank Lloyd Wright for Kids.* Chicago Review Press, 1994

Frank Lloyd Wright: A Film by Ken Burns and Lynn Novick. 1998

Alexander Calder

Baal-Teshuva, Jacob and Calder, Alexander. *Calder: 1989–1976.* TASCHEN America, 1998.

Guerrero, Pedro E. *Calder at Home: The Joyous Environment of Alexander Calder.* Stewart, Tabori & Chang. 1998.

Venezia, Mike. *Alexander Calder (Getting To Know the World's Greatest Artists).* Children's Press, 1999.

American Masters Present Alexander Calder. PBS, 60 minutes. 1998.

Mobile by Alexander Calder (A National Gallery of Art Presentation). Home Vision Arts.

Georgia O'Keeffe

Castro, Jan Garden. *The Art & Life of Georgia O'Keeffe.* Crown Publishing, 1995.

Lisle, Laurie. *Portrait of an Artist: A Biography of Georgia O'Keeffe.* Washington Square Press, 1997.

Robinson, Roxana and O'Keeffe, Georgia. *Georgia O'Keeffe: A Life.* University Press of New England, 1999.

Turner, Robyn Montana. *Georgia O'Keeffe—Portraits of Women Artists for Children.* Little Brown and Co., 1991.

Portrait of an Artist: Georgia O'Keeffe. Homevision, 2000.

Art Resources *(cont.)*

Grant Wood

Duggleby, John. *Artist in Overalls: The Life of Grant Wood.* Chronicle Books, 1996.

Graham, Nan Wood, Zug, John, and Julie Jensen McDonald. *My Brother, Grant Wood.* State Historical Society Iowa, 1993.

Thomas, Jennifer. *Masterpiece of the Month (Grades K-5).* Teacher Created Resources Inc., 2001.

Venezia, Mike. *Grant Wood (Getting to Know the World's Greatest Artists).* Children's Press, 1996.

Wood, Grant (Ed.), et al. *Grant Wood: An American Master Revealed.* Pomegranate, 1996.

Dorothea Lange

Meltzer, Milton. *Dorothea Lange: A Photographer's Life.* Syracuse University Press, 2000.

Partridge, Elizabeth and Lange, Dorothea. *Restless Spirit: The Life and Work of Dorothea Lange.* Viking Children's Books, 1998.

Turner, Robyn Montana. *Portraits of Women Artists for Children, Dorothea Lange.* Little Brown and Co., 1994.

Venezia, Mike. *Dorothea Lange (Getting to Know the World's Greatest Artists).* Children's Press, 2001.

Walt Disney

Green, Amy Boothe and Green, Howard E. *Remembering Walt: Favorite Memories of Walt Disney.* Hyperion, 1999.

Mosley, Leonard. *Disney's World: A Biography.* Scarborough House, 1990.

Thomas, Bob. *Walt Disney: An American Original.* Hyperion, 1994.

Norman Rockwell

Finch, Charles S., et. al. *Norman Rockwell's America.* Abradale Press, 1994.

Hennessey, Maureen Hart (Ed.). *Norman Rockwell: Pictures for the American People.* 1999.

Rockwell, Norman, et al. *Norman Rockwell: My Adventures as an Illustrator.* Harry N. Abrams, 1995.

Louise Nevelson

Kohl, MaryAnne F. and Solga, Kim. *Discovering Great Artists: Hands-On Art for Children in the Styles of the Great Masters.* Bright Ring Publishing, 1997.

Lisle, Laurie. *Louise Nevelson: A Passionate Life.* Washington Square Press, 1991.

Louise Nevelson in Process. 29 minutes. 1987.

Jackson Pollock

Frank, Elizabeth. *Jackson Pollock (Modern Masters Series, Vol. 3).* Abbeville Press, Inc., 1983.

Spring, Justin. *The Essential Jackson Pollock.* Andrews McMeel Publishing, 1998.

Venezia, Mike. *Jackson Pollock (Getting to Know the World's Greatest Artists).* Children's Press, 1994.

Jackson Pollock. 1987.

Portrait of an Artist: Jackson Pollock—Ideas in Paint. 1992.

Andy Warhol

Baal-Teshuva, Jacob. *Andy Warhol, 1928–1987.* Prestel USA, 1993.

Francis, Mark, et al. *Andy Warhol: Drawings 1942–1987.* Bullfinch Press, 1999.

Tretiack, Phillippe, et al. *Andy Warhol (Universe of Art).* Vendome Press, 1997.

Venezia, Mike. *Andy Warhol (Getting to Know the World's Greatest Artists).* Children's Press, 1996.

Warhol. 79 minutes. 1987

Art Resources *(cont.)*

Judy Chicago

Lucie-Smith, Edward and Chicago, Judy. *Judy Chicago: An American Vision.* Watson-Guptill Publications, 2000.

Lucie-Smith, Edward and Chicago, Judy. *Women and Art: Contested Territory.* Watson-Guptill Publications, 1999.

Faith Ringgold

Ringgold, Faith. *We Flew Over the Bridge: The Memories of Faith Ringgold.* Little, Brown, 1995.

Ringgold, Faith., Freeman, Linda., and Roucher, Nancy. *Talking to Faith Ringgold.* Crown Publishers, 1995.

Chuck Close

Close, Chuck. *Chuck Close.* Bookpeople, 1983.

Greenberg, Jan and Jordan, Sandra. *Chuck Close Up Close.* DK Publishing, 2000.

Storr, Robert, et al. *Chuck Close.* Harry N. Abrams, 1998.

Westerbeck, Colin. *Chuck Close.* Art Institute of Chicago Museum, 1989.

Chuck Close: A Portrait in Progress. 1998.

Maya Lin

Lin, Maya. *Boundaries.* Simon & Schuster, 2000.

Ling, Bettina. *Maya Lin (Contemporary Biographies).* Raintree/Steck Vaughn, 1997.

Yokoe, Lynn. *Maya Lin, Architect.* Modern Curriculum Press, 1995.

Maya Lin: A Strong Clear Vision. 1995.

Judith Baca

Cockcroft, Eva Sperling and Barnet-Sanchez, Holly. *Signs from the Heart: California Chicano Murals.* University of New Mexico Press, 1993.

Novas, Himilce. *Everything You Need to Know About Latino History.* Penguin Putnam, 1994.

Luis Jimenez

Artman, John. *Cowboys: An Activity Book.* Good Apple, Inc., 1982.

Flores-Turney, Camille. *Howl: The Artwork of Luis Jimenez (New Mexico Magazine Artist Series).* University of New Mexico Press, 1998.

Jimenez, Luis, et al. *Man on Fire.* University of New Mexico Press, 1994.

Lippard, Lucy R. *Luis Jimenez.* Albuquerque Museum of Art, History and Science, 1994.

George Lucas

Lucas, George and Kline, Sally (Ed.). *George Lucas: Interview (Conversations with Filmmakers Series).* University Press of Mississippi, 1999.

Pollock, Dale. Skywalking: *The Life and Films of George Lucas.* Da Capo Press, 1999.

Rau, Dana Meachen and Rau, Christopher. *George Lucas Creator of Star Wars.* Franklin Watts, 1999.

General References

Berry, Nancy L., et al. *Experience Art: A Handbook for Teaching and Learning with Works of Art.* Crystal Productions, 1996.

Cavanaugh, Betty Gaglio. *Multicultural Art Activities.* Teacher Created Resources, Inc., 1994.

Cook, J. *Understanding Modern Art.* EDC Publications, 1992.

Janson, W. W. and Janson, Anthony E. *History of Art for Young People.* Harry N. Abrams, Inc., 1992.

Madoff, S. Henry. *POP Art a Critical History.* University of California, Berkeley Press, 1997

Ross, Stewart. *Oxford Children's Book of the 20th Century.* Oxford University Press, 1998.

Thompson, Kimberly Boehler and Loftus, Diana Standing. *Art Connections: Integrating Art Throughout the Curriculum.* GoodYear Books, 1995.

Time Line Cards

Eadweard Muybridge

Frederic Remington

Alfred Stieglitz

Frank Lloyd Wright

Alexander
Calder

Georgia
O'Keeffe

Grant Wood

Dorothea Lange

Walt Disney

Norman
Rockwell

Louise
Nevelson

Jackson
Pollock

Andy Warhol

Judy Chicago

Faith Ringgold

Chuck Close

Maya Lin

Judith Baca

Luis Jimenez

George Lucas